SUPREMELY SUCCESSFUL SELLING

DISCOVERING THE MAGIC INGREDIENT

JEROLD PANAS

WILEY

John Wiley & Sons, Inc.

The Joy of Selling!

A salesman stood at the heavenly gate,
His face was scarred and old.
He stood before the man of fate
For admission to the fold.
"What have you done," Saint Peter said,
"To gain admission here."
"I've been a salesman, sir," he said,
"For many and many a year."
The pearly gates swung open wide,
Saint Peter rang the bell.
"Come in and choose your harp," he sighed—
"You've had your share of hell!"

Contents

v

1

A Charmed and Fulfilling Life

CONGRATULATIONS.

You are among the most highly esteemed and privileged. You are a partner in one of life's most noble professions. All of the world's commerce depends on you.

You are the power that turns the axle that spins the wheel that moves the shaft that activates the lever that fires the steam that drives the engine. You are the engine that makes it all happen.

You are a salesperson—among a select group who experience what George Bernard Shaw praised as: "The joy of being used for a purpose recognized by all as a mighty one."

You've shown your eagerness to call on others for a product of importance to the buyer. You talk with friends, business colleagues, and even some people you don't know well.

That's what makes selling and your involvement so vitally important. And, at the same time, so immensely rewarding and exciting.

Your work is vital. Without you, your company couldn't exist. It couldn't sell its product, make a profit, provide its services, employ its people. You make it possible.

And your task is fun. Yes, just plain fun. You are one with Jack Welch, former CEO of General Electric: "I don't like this job. I love it." You make a good living. Best of all, it's fulfilling.

Everyone you call on will have a distinct feeling about buying, and have a different perception of your product. Each person will be in a different position financially, will vary in her attraction for your product. She will send changing buying signals. She will bring to the situation and the purchase her unique stresses and strains, joys and high spirits. And a tangled web of motivations regarding the purchase.

You will find no presentation is the same as the next. And I can almost promise you that none will follow the exact scenario you plan.

But that's not important. Because what I've discovered in all my years of selling is that it seldom matters how you ask—although I'll give you important tips and suggestions in this book. What is important is that you ask for the order. Just do it. Ask for the order!

There's no such thing as an incorrect ask. Yes, you read that correctly.

Maybe it could have been done more effectively or more strategically. Perhaps with more finesse and style. But what matters most is that you ask.

That's what really counts. And you do it with enthusiasm and commitment.

"Success in selling is simply enthusiasm and persistence in action," Mary Kay Ash told me once, "I want my salespeople to be driven, enthusiastic, and energetic, and passionate. Yes, passionate about our products."

Just remember—selling is a contact sport! I've learned that no matter how dazzling your presentation, not everyone will buy. Or the purchase may not be at the level you hoped.

This can be disappointing. I know. I've been there, when parts of me are clenched tight enough to crack walnuts.

The pain can be so great it can hurt you into poetry! But what keeps you going is that you did your best.

In my coaching, I tell the men and women in my seminars to simply remember this great truth:

SW SW SW SW

Some Will. Some Won't. So What! Someone's Waiting.

That's the important lesson. Not everyone will buy. But there's a whole world of people waiting for you to call on them.

On the pages that follow, you will discover the magic ingredient of supremely successful selling. What you read may surprise you.

Have you ever noticed that often the most profound matters are those you have been staring at all along and haven't yet recognized? You suddenly—aha!—come upon it.

It will remind you of Sherlock Holmes telling Watson: "It was there all the time, dear fellow, just waiting for you to discover it. You must learn my methods."

You will find it here, in this book. I provide the catechism of selling. You will discover something unusual is happening here. Just learn my methods.

Congratulations. Get ready for the great adventure. Selling is what I call, "a life poured into words and passion."

Because of you and the sales you make, you'll be directly responsible, through your product, for touching lives. For many you are calling on, you are bringing joy and satisfaction. You are making it happen.

In truth, successful salespeople attain a kind of immortality. It is impossible to know if their influence ever stops. If it ever does.

2 | The Great Ones

HERE IS A ROSTER of some of the extraordinary men and women you will meet in the pages that follow. They are listed here in the order they appear in the book.

I guess just about the whole world knows the name **Mary Kay**. You met her in the first chapter. Today, the company she founded has over 1 million salespeople in 30 different countries.

Mary Kay Ash started the company because . . . well because she was darn angry! She was fuming because in the job she had right out of high school, men had all the breaks. It was impossible for a woman to get a promotion.

So this determined young woman founded Mary Kay Cosmetics Inc. It was a rather presumptuous name for a one-employee firm. She began by selling door to door. Mary Kay is a superb salesperson and her company grew. And grew.

She is a mesmerizing speaker and a remarkable coach. Attend one of her meetings where she invites her top salespeople (almost all women) and you are ready to give up your present job and knock yourself out to get the pink Cadillac she awards her top salespeople.

Her firm is founded on the Golden Rule. She says honesty and integrity are the cornerstones of her growth.

Alan G. Hassenfeld is the high-energy board chairman of Hasbro Inc. The company is a worldwide leader in children's toys and family entertainment. He recently retired as CEO. The corporation has revenue of over $4 billion.

He began his career at the corporation in 1970 and worked his way through the ranks. At one time, he carried the major responsibility for worldwide marketing and sales. He finally took charge in 1989 as CEO. During his tenure, Hasbro doubled in revenue.

He estimates he has worked with over 700 salespeople. His antennae are finely tuned to what is essential in selling. Alan is credited with taking the company into international operations.

His sales and management attributes are widely recognized. The list of those who seek his counsel is long. This includes some of the nation's largest and most highly regarded corporations. He was named by Rhode Island College's Business School to its Hall of Fame.

Melanie Sabelhaus is a force to be reckoned with. She has the power to blow the windows open. The first thing you notice about her is the extraordinary vitality. She has so much energy she makes coffee nervous.

She was one of IBM's most successful salespeople and headed the national Office Products Division. She then started her own company, which offered temporary housing. Before it went public, she supervised 75 salespeople in her role as CEO.

She was asked by President George W. Bush to be second in command of the Small Business Administration—involving thousands of salespeople.

Melanie knows a thing or two about sales.

Dortch Oldman was president and major stockholder in the Southwestern Company. The firm engages thousands of college students each summer to sell religious and educational books door to door. Door to door! That's tough selling.

Dortch is one of the nation's greatest mentors of young salespeople. He has trained thousands.

The company has 130,000 alumni. The group represents some of today's most prominent national leaders. Its mission is to help young people earn their way through college. In their training, they are taught that persistence is essential—but nothing is more important than selling with integrity.

Stanley Marcus is the sales genius who transformed his grandfather's fur store in Dallas into one of the nation's premier department stores. You now find a Neiman Marcus store in virtually every high-end shopping center and mall in the country.

Neiman-Marcus was launched with an original investment of $25,000. Because of its extraordinary service and the coaching of its salespeople, it became the darling of Dallas society. And then it simply expanded from there to all over the world.

Stanley Marcus was named Salesman of the Century by *Fortune* magazine. He has received virtually every major citation and tribute awarded by the sales profession. He is a selling *shaman* and has influenced every salesperson in his empire, first in the Dallas store, and then in all his stores.

After retiring, he spent the next dozen years as a marketing and sales consultant to some of the nation's largest corporations and retail stores. Well into his late 80s, he flew from coast to coast to dispense his wisdom.

He was my friend and my mentor. He wrote the foreword for one of my books.

Malin Burnham is chairman emeritus of one of the largest commercial real estate and insurance brokerages in the country. In his tenure as CEO, he supervised hundreds of salespeople.

He takes his corporate life seriously. But he finds time, also, to be on the crew of the winning boat in the America's Cup, continue his daily game of handball (triple-A champion), and be San Diego's leading can-do citizen. If it's something that's good for San Diego, he is leading the pack.

Malin has led every major fundraising campaign in San Diego. If you think that doesn't take selling, you don't understand fundraising! There's a building at Stanford that carries his name and one of the nation's leading medical research centers is named the Sanford–Burnham Institute.

Mary Ellen Rodgers is the national managing partner for field operations for Deloitte & Touche. In that position she is in charge of over 3,500 employees.

The firm is one of the world's largest in services for auditing, management consulting, and financial counsel. Mary Ellen is a member of Deloitte's operating committee. Those who know her predict this is not the end of her meteoric rise.

Her previous position was heading the Western Michigan office of the firm. In that post, she increased the billings by a factor of six in only a few years. An extraordinary sales achievement.

Deloitte is a service firm. And that requires a very special type of selling to acquire new clients. No easy task! You are selling an intangible that requires your integrity, experience, and yes—ideas.

Thomas Shores founded Classic Leather in Hickory, North Carolina. It grew from a small garage operation into one of the largest manufacturers in the nation of luxury leather furniture.

His designs are breathtaking. When you compare them with the competition, even though they are twice the cost, you have to choose the Classic Leather line.

The colors are bewitching, to fit any décor and enhance any room. The furniture somehow captures the spirit of the family. Great workmanship and leather as soft as melted butter.

The quality of the furniture is all part of the company's success. But there's more. Tommy has performed magic with his sales staff. They are the best coached in this highly competitive field.

Richard DeVos founded the Amway Corporation with his lifelong friend and business partner, the late Jay Van Andel. I doubt they had any idea that their modest beginning would end up being an $8 billion worldwide corporation.

Amway, if you didn't already know, is a direct-selling company that now operates in 80 countries and territories around the world. There are three million people who sell for the company and own their own independent business.

Rich DeVos is a captivating motivational speaker. Listen to him for 30 minutes and you're ready to become an Amway representative! Over his 50 years of involvement with the company, there are literally hundreds of thousands of salespeople whose lives he has touched. And hundreds (hundreds!) he has made millionaires.

He is the author of four books, all best sellers. His latest is called, *Ten Powerful Phrases for Powerful People*. It focuses on integrity, having a positive attitude, and encouraging others to live a fuller life.

From his beginning, selling Nutrilite (a food supplement) to the now extraordinary growth of the corporation, Rich has lived a fulfilling and rewarding life. In the past 50 years, he has been a close friend of every U.S. president and meets regularly with the two George Bushes and Bill Clinton. His recorded talk, "Selling America," received the Alexander Hamilton Award from the Freedoms Foundation.

Bonnie McElveen Hunter is owner and CEO of Pace Communications. It is the nation's leader in developing custom content programs for some of the world's most prominent and recognizable brands.

Just out of college, she began selling advertising—and quickly became the company's leading salesperson. She kept selling and was so successful, she soon bought the company. She has never stopped selling.

She and her 250 design and sales staff are the industry's most highly regarded in what is a fiercely competitive field. "Innovate selling" would best describe their magic mantra. Pace Communications is ranked by *Working Woman* magazine as one of the nation's top women-owned businesses.

Bonnie is former U.S. ambassador to Finland. She currently serves as chairman of the American Red Cross, the first woman to be elected chair in the organization's 100-plus-year history. She is a founder of the United Way Billion Dollar National Women's Leadership Initiative.

Cal Turner Jr. began his career at Dollar General nearly 45 years ago. It was a company that was co-founded in 1939 by his father and grandfather. He succeeded his father as president in 1977 and became chairman 10 years later.

When he took over the company, there were 125 stores. He has built the company into an organization with more than 6,000 stores in 27 states. There are annual sales in excess of $6 billion.

It is a major retail enterprise. All together there are well over 65,000 salespeople and managers involved in the organization. Cal was responsible for the coaching and success of this group.

In addition to being considered an astute and effective manager, he is considered a brilliant salesman. One-on-one, he is totally captivating. Irresistible! He captures lightning in a bottle.

In addition to his 14-hour-a-day schedule and running the business, he has found time to chair a dozen national and regional nonprofits, including several colleges and universities.

W. Clement Stone grew up in Chicago's tough South Side. His father left home when he was three. To help support his family, he began selling newspapers on the street at the age of six.

When older boys drove him away from the busiest corners, he moved his sales to restaurants and office buildings. Even at that early age, the seeds were sown for the formation of what became one of the largest insurance companies in the country.

He never finished high school. Instead, he worked with his mother selling accident policies. He had enormous success cold-canvassing office buildings, one floor to the next.

Stone started Combined Insurance Co. with an investment of $100. He began adding salespeople. He coached them, one by one, in his sales methods and techniques. The company grew into a billion-dollar enterprise.

He is the author of three best-selling inspirational books. His success is based on the philosophy of maintaining a Positive Mental Attitude. Every time I met with him, he was quick to tell me that all he wanted to do was change the world.

Clem Stone is a limited edition. By that I mean, there's nobody quite like him. There never was. There never will be.

3

Failure Is the Path
of Least Persistence

FOR ME, one of the great joys I have is knowing my product is providing a real service to the buyer. For many, it brings enormous satisfaction and touches their lives in surprising ways I can't even imagine.

There isn't another profession that can offer the same personal rewards and inner glow. You are helping the buyers secure something of importance to them. At times, it is something they had hoped and dreamed about—whether the purchase is large or small.

I find that the really difficult part of selling isn't in getting people to buy. That's actually easy. I give you the fail-proof guidelines in this book. The tough part for many is asking for the order.

But, as you'll learn in these pages, asking for the order shouldn't cause trembling and a timid heart. Effective selling isn't flimflam huckstering or razzle-dazzle peddling. Or bargaining and gibberish. And it certainly isn't persuading someone to do something he doesn't want to do.

"In the salesman, I look for integrity first." That's what Alan Hassenfeld tells me. "You want to become a partner with the buyer. You're not just selling a product. You need to know you're benefiting the buyer. That's selling with integrity." Precisely. It's selling with integrity. That's what you will be dealing with in this book. That's the magic ingredient. Integrity.

It means encouraging people to take action for something that in the end is good for them. Or brings them enjoyment and gives them pleasure. It can't be just a win for you, the salesman. That's not integrity selling. It must be a win-win.

Keep in mind that there will be some who don't want to buy your product. Or at least on first blush don't see how it will benefit them. You're never a loser until you quit trying.

It's your job to help the buyer understand how great the advantage. You assure them of the value of the product in their personal life or the company they work for.

You don't bamboozle them into buying. That's not integrity selling.

"After you strip away everything else, all you have left is the salesperson's integrity," says Melanie Sabelhaus. "If there isn't integrity on the part of the salesperson, nothing else matters."

People don't want to spend money. But they are willing to pay the price for a fair exchange—your product for their dollars. You help them make the choice.

Don't worry about theatrical techniques and flashy tools. In fact, I don't spend a lot of time on that in this book.

What is far more important is having the right instincts. You keep your antennae quivering during the entire meeting with the buyer. Listen more than you talk. Positive results follow. I promise.

And by the way, I don't like the word *prospect*. I have stricken it from my vocabulary. I much prefer the words *likely buyer*. Doesn't that sound better, more confident? Doesn't that get the person one step closer to buying your product?

I'll never use the word *prospect* again. Follow my lead.

And as for that horrible word *suspect*—I have buried that word forever. It's demeaning. Let's refer to that person as a *possible buyer*. Doesn't that feel more positive? More affirming?

One of your jobs is to get the possible buyer to become a likely buyer. And then, of course, a buyer.

Don't be concerned about not being an expert at selling. You will be. Keep in mind that the *Titanic* was built by an expert and Noah's Ark by a rank amateur.

In his career, Michael Jordan said he missed nearly 10,000 shots, lost over 3,000 games, and missed making the decisive shot in a game dozens of times. "I've failed over and over in my life . . . and that is why I succeeded."

On those occasions when you don't make the sale—and there will be those times—it likely won't be your execution that fails. You'll give it your best. Your presentation will be nothing short of dazzling and you'll ask for the order. You won't stumble, say the wrong things, or fail to follow the script. None of that.

Some men and women simply will not buy. That's not your failure. It's their loss.

One day, I asked my friend Dortch Oldman what gave him the greatest reward with the thousands of salespeople he has trained. "It's teaching college students that hard work and persistence pays handsomely.

"And they need to know that through their sales they are enriching the lives of those who buy the books. That's essential. If it's not the right thing for the family, it's not the right thing for us.

"I am careful to tell them that making a sale is not important if they compromise their integrity. I advise them to promise much—and to keep their promises. Exceed expectations.

"I tell them they are rare and privileged. They make a great difference in the lives of those they call on. I explain that selling is one of the greatest professions in the world."

You are an ethical ambassador for your product. You are in a virtuous profession. You are enriching lives.

You understand that everyone—no matter what their profession, job, or status is—is in the business of selling. You understand better than anyone that everything in life is selling.

4 | Move Those Marbles

I HAD JUST FINISHED SPEAKING. If I do say so myself, it was one of my better days. The group was responsive, they laughed in the proper places. I ended with something I felt had somewhat the resounding impact of Tchaikovsky's *1812 Overture*.

People were on their feet applauding. Wow! A standing ovation. It was a blessed moment. As Tennessee Williams said: "I felt as though I had just inherited the sky."

In a sense, these were my kind of people. It was a meeting of 500 or so men and women. I'd led them through two full days of an exhausting seminar. I was bone-tired but exhilarated with the response I received.

I finished my speech by telling the group that selling is more than a profession. It's a way of life.

If you're not selling, people aren't buying. And if they're not, there's no commerce. Everything comes to a standstill. It's your selling that makes things happen.

When the applause died down, Milton Murray, master of ceremonies, got up to thank me.

"Jerry, you've meant so much to so many of us in the last two days. The group got together and decided to do something special for you. We're going to name a chair in your honor."

A chair! A named chair. In my honor. I was stunned.

I knew I'd have to respond in some way. But as I began pushing my chair back to stand, there wasn't a single thought in my mind. A total blank. All I could think of was the admonition: "Forget the cheese—just find a way to get out of the trap."

Milton continued talking as I walked toward the podium to accept my honor.

"Well, it isn't exactly a chair," he said. From behind the table, Milton produced a three-legged stool and waved it high above his head.

I looked at Milton and the stool. ("Cripes, what's this all about?")

"It's just what it looks like, Jerry. It's a milking stool. And on it is a brass plaque in your honor. We're giving you this because you've taught us so well."

By this time, I had reached the podium. Milton was congratulating me and pumping my hand. He read the plaque. It turned out to be what I consider a salesman's credo. The plaque read:

You don't get milk from a cow by sending a letter. And you don't get milk by calling on the phone. The only way to get milk from a cow is to sit by its side and milk it.

Let this be a lesson to you. Remember it well.

You won't make a sale, at least not of any size, by sending a letter. And you won't make a sale by calling on the telephone, not of the size you want.

To make a sale at the level you want, you're going to have to call on the likely buyer in person.

Sit by that cow and milk it!

At one of my seminars, I asked everyone to think of the person who was their role model, someone who had left an indelible mark on their life.

A few told their story. Then Bob got up. He was vice president at the University of Tennessee. I'll never forget his story. And lesson.

Bob began talking about his father. "Dad was the best friend I ever had. I miss him terribly.

"He taught me to ride a bike and how to hit a baseball. We went fishing together and camping."

For some reason I can't to this day explain, I thought there might be a teachable moment for the group. So I started asking Bob some questions.

"It's obvious your dad was an inspiration to you, Bob. What did your father do for a living?"

"He sold life insurance," Bob said. (Aha. I'm thinking I'm on to something! I'll keep probing.)

"Was your father successful?" I ask.

"He sold for Prudential Life Insurance. Five years he led the Southeast region for his company, and one year he led the whole country."

"I bet I know how he made all those sales," I said. "He sent letters to a bunch of people and asked them to buy his life insurance."

"Good grief, no," Bob replied. "People don't sell life insurance by writing letters."

"How dumb of me. Of course not. He probably got to the office early and called them on the phone and asked them to buy his insurance."

"You're still wrong," Bob said.

(Wait until you read what Bob told the group. It's fascinating.)

"Well, what did he do to sell so much insurance?" I ask. Bob responded with this story.

"When Dad got up in the morning, he put four marbles in his right-hand pocket. During the day, when he called on someone and actually spoke about life insurance and asked them to buy a policy, he would move a marble from the right-hand pocket to the left.

"Not over a cocktail, not at Rotary, not in the parking lot—but only when he sat down with someone and asked them to buy a policy. When the visit was over, he would move a marble from the right- to the left-hand pocket.

"And Dad didn't come home in the evening until he had moved all his marbles."

Let that be the anthem you sing. You have to move those marbles.

5 | It's Never Too Late to Be What You Might Have Been

WHAT ARE THE FACTORS that make you successful and effective as a salesperson?

Is it hyper-selling? Is it your ability to induce someone to buy your product by the sheer weight of your eloquence and an astonishing flow of words? Sales drivel and chatter? Oogah-boogah?

Or did you make the sale because you overpromised? Or you overwhelmed the likely buyer? There are some people who just don't like to say *no*.

I'm certain it isn't any of these offensive approaches. But I wanted to know. I wanted a finite answer to what makes a great salesperson.

So I conducted a number of focus groups. Here's the nature of the questions I probed:

- What can you remember about the man or woman who called on you (whether a friend, relative, casual acquaintance, or someone you didn't know)? What qualities stand out most in your mind?
- What is it that made that person an effective salesperson? Assume the product is something you like and the price is about right. What was it about the solicitor you liked most? What impressed you most?
- Let's say you are considering two different products. Both are similar in price, apparent quality, aesthetically pleasing, and comparable—the same in just about every respect. Tell me, why did you choose the product you did?

You will grant me these are three penetrating questions. Incisive. Acute. Thought provoking.

Here's what I found. I call them my Four Es: empathy, energy, enthusiasm, and ethics.

These are the qualities the men and women in my focus groups all agreed they looked for. There were other essential elements, of course. But even if I added everything else together, they were less influential than these Four Es. So note them well.

Your buyers need to be heard. They need to feel you are listening. That's how you become empathetic. It is one of the most powerful motivating forces in human nature.

"It was one of the most important days of my life," Thoreau wrote in his journal. "I spoke and someone listened."

The men and women I queried in our focus groups give very high marks to a salesperson who listens. Truly listens. The salesperson spiritually enters into the buyer's world and experience. Spirit and heart.

What I'm going to tell you next may seem counterintuitive. In the studies we conduct, we find men and women buy emotionally. The determination is seldom cerebral. It is visceral. The decision goes from the heart to the wallet.

I was reminded just the other day how listening is directly linked to empathy. I was digging through an old file and came across a newspaper clipping I've saved for years. The date was 1933.

It's a photograph of Franklin Roosevelt in his familiar crushed fedora. He is leaning heavily on his cane. He is bent markedly forward, listening intently to two ragged men, perhaps homeless, who appear to have stopped him. He is leaning close to them. The caption underneath the photograph reads: "He knows how to listen."

That's your role as a salesperson—to listen. And that's how people in our focus groups identified empathy. They want you to get to know them. Your probable buyers want to be heard!

Studies are clear on the subject. Unambiguous. People are drawn to and charmed by those who listen to them.

I love this story about Lady Marlborough. She was invited on two different evenings in the same week to a royal dinner. At the first, she was seated next to former Prime Minister Gladstone. A few days later she sat next to Benjamin Disraeli, then the current prime minister. What was it like, she was asked by a friend, to sit next to and dine with two of England's most prominent men?

"Well," she said, "Sitting next to Gladstone, I thought he was the most important person in the entire world. Sitting next to Disraeli, I thought I was the most important person in the world."

There's an astonishing transformation that takes place when you listen. The more you listen, the more you find out about your likely buyer. More important, if you listen carefully, very carefully, you know precisely what motivates the buyer.

Be certain you listen, also, with your eyes. One of the important things in selling is to hear what isn't being said.

People don't care how much you know until they know how much you care about them. When you're calling on someone, you don't want them thinking you view them only as a dollar sign—someone you're going to sell something to. That's not integrity selling.

Next of the Four Es is energy. Time and time again in the focus groups, participants talked about the energy their favorite salesmen brought to the visit. They said there were sparks that ignite the spirit.

The most powerful weapon on earth is the human soul on fire. It's what Robert Frost called "that immense energy of life which sparks a fire."

I find this true in all successful salespeople. There's a highly charged energy. You feel surrounded by it. Like being in the eye of a tornado, and there's no way of escaping.

The really effective salespeople seem to have an internal reservoir of vitality and dash. They're able to bring forth a torrent of energy. Even when they've had an exhausting day.

These are the kind of people who, when they seem to be at the end of their rope—simply tie a knot in it and hang on. They forge on for unlimited periods.

Stanley Marcus told me that selling takes a great deal of energy. He gives high marks to those who are able to go beyond fatigue and distress, and find a new source of power and vigor they never dreamed they had.

Our focus group said the callers they liked best of all seemed to be peak performers, filled with effervescent energy. They told me that the salesperson's energy is infectious.

They say they feel the energy. And the buyer feeds it back. It becomes a spiritual feast.

"I insist on integrity in my salespeople. But next comes energy." That's what Melanie Sabelhaus told me.

"Unlimited energy. Then I want them to be passionate about their product. Most of all, they must have deep respect for the buyer—and I consider that as having integrity."

Actually, when people in our focus groups singled out energy, they were not talking about nervous activity. They are drawn to someone who is incandescent, who lights up like a bulb when talking about their product. Someone with the kind of energy that exudes passion and joy.

Enthusiasm is the third E. Everyone in my focus groups spoke about it. It's probably the ingredient that is the most telling and effective in the asking-buying mix.

Enthusiasm comes from two Greek words. *En* comes from the Greek, meaning within. And *thusiasm* from the Greek word *theos*—God. To be enthusiastic, therefore, is to have God within you. That seems to be what all of the groups characterized as being an essential ingredient of a successful salesperson.

Passion! If you don't have that for your product, find a new product.

Unbridled, unflinching, unbounded enthusiasm—the successful salespeople are imbued with it. Like a soup bowl filled to the brim and spilling over.

A magnificent presentation, dazzling literature, even a great product—none of this matters if there isn't enthusiasm. It's what Melanie called "working near the heart of things."

Enthusiasm is contagious. Start an epidemic.

Empathy. Energy. Enthusiasm. It's your job to bring these qualities to the solicitation.

But there is one last factor. Everyone we interviewed spoke of it. Everyone!

They told us they can *feel* it. It permeates everything the salesperson does and says. They are clear. That irrefutable attribute is—ethics.

You never tamper with the truth.

This is hardly new. In Deuteronomy, 4,000 years ago, Moses tells the men and women of Israel: "Don't try to cheat people by having two sets of weights or measures—one to get more when you're selling and one to pay less when you're buying. Don't let yourself be taken in by smooth talk. Don't have people around you like that."

Integrity is the mightiest weapon in the salesman's arsenal—more important than any literature about the product or anything that is said by the salesperson. The power of integrity is explosive. No matter how dazzling your presentation.

David Hirsch was CEO and owner of Vertox, one of the world's largest manufacturers of metal fasteners. In reality, nuts and bolts. He just sold the company.

"Nuts and bolts! Isn't that just plain taking an order?" I ask him.

What do you think David tells me is the most important attribute for the nearly 100 salespeople he employed? "Integrity leads the list," he says.

Malin Burnham agrees.

"Even if I really like the product and it makes good sense for me, and let's say the price is right—if I don't have confidence in the person calling on me, if I have any concern about ethics, there's no sale.

"I can feel it. I can almost touch it. If I question the integrity of the person, there's no sale. The session closes. Good-bye!"

In selling, integrity is *sine qua non*—the essential ingredient. Integrity must be a part of the salesperson's DNA.

Ethics alone is no assurance of making the sale. But without it, you can't even begin the journey. You are a canon, ready to be fired—but without ammunition.

This book is all about selling and motivating your buyer. But woven throughout the entire fabric of each chapter is the thread of integrity. Integrity isn't important—it is everything.

If the buyers can't believe the messenger, they won't believe the message.

6

There Are Really No Mistakes in Selling—Only Lessons

TWO EXPLORERS in the deepest African jungle are captured by a wild tribe. They are surrounded. The chief confronts them and says, "I give you the choice: death or kee-kee."

The first explorer, reasoning that nothing can be worse than death, elects kee-kee. This turns out to be a protracted form of horrible torture and mutilation.

The chief then offers the second explorer the same choice.

"I choose death," he says with resignation.

"Very well—death," says the chief. "But first kee-kee."

The truth is . . . well, the truth is that in selling there are times you're not certain whether to choose death or kee-kee. You won't make every sale. I don't.

When I was just beginning my career, I somehow managed to get an appointment with Crawford H. Greenewalt. He was CEO of DuPont.

My sales presentation was perfectly rehearsed and delivered. I felt it was just short of being brilliant. Somewhere in the background, I thought I could hear the theme from *Rocky*.

When I finished he said: "Young man, I want to give you a lesson I hope you won't forget. In the 45 minutes we were together, you didn't find out a single thing about me. You didn't find out what I'm interested in, and you didn't ask any questions. You spent all of your time hard selling. I like to buy, but I don't like to be sold. Learn to understand the difference and you can be a success."

I didn't make the sale. I was disappointed, of course. I discovered that experience is what you get when you are expecting something else.

I learned the lesson Greenewalt taught me. Now I try to be as subtle as a watermark.

If you make enough calls, you're going to meet and talk with a number of wonderful men and women. You are on a captivating expedition. That's part of the reward of being a salesperson.

I love them all, everyone I call on. Even those who don't buy. (Well . . . okay, okay! Perhaps those who turn me down, I love a little less.)

I learn something from every call and contact I make. You will, also. The sales profession provides an exciting journey—where at every intersection, challenge meets opportunity.

One of the lessons I've learned is that there are five levels of buyers. If you understand these five categories, you will find there are actually some men and women you won't want to contact after the first or second call.

I want this to be part of your sales creed. Begin putting your contacts in one of these levels. Just remember, however, that every successful sale begins with the decision to try.

One of the best ways I find to describe the levels is to think of a pot of water on your range. I call what follows my Heat Index.

Boiling. This is an enlightened buyer. They will purchase your product without much of a presentation—barely any discussion at all. Many times, they will initiate the contact with you. (Inspiring the same feeling Beethoven must have had in mind when he wrote "Ode to Joy".)

Your job is to keep these folks forever cultivated and informed. I call this process stewardship. And this is what's important. You can freely ask these people to give you the names of friends, neighbors, or associates you can call on. They will give you permission to use them as references.

Let me tell you something about stewardship. It's the activity of reminding people, on a regular basis, of how important they are to you. Like a kaleidoscope—to be shown appreciation in a thousand different forms and ways.

I'll give you an interesting example of what I have in mind. I'll never forget the moment. I was at a meeting with a client. We were interrupted.

The receptionist came into the room and told me I had a telephone call from the president of American Airlines. (Good grief! The president of American Airlines!)

The client was impressed. "The president of American Airlines. For heaven's sake. Take the call. Take the call." I took the call.

"Hello Jerry Panas. This is Bob Crandall, president of American Airlines. You have just reached the two-million-mile mark with our airline, and I just wanted to thank you for your loyalty. You are so important to us."

That took, how long, no more than 30 seconds. Did it make me a fan of American Airlines? You bet. For life.

But it didn't stop there. About every six months, I get a letter from the vice president of sales thanking me for my continued use of the airline.

Next in importance to asking for and making the sale is providing stewardship. Your job is not to make a sale. It is to make a friend and a life-long customer.

Very Hot. These men and women will buy your product and will require very little persuasion. They are ready! All they require from you is a little explanation.

You can also ask these folks to be a reference for you and suggest who among their friends you might call on.

Hot. These folks will buy, but they need to be persuaded— at times intensely. But they will buy. Your effective salesmanship and integrity will carry the day.

Keep in mind the job of the salesperson is not to take the horse to water and make it drink. The salesperson's job is to make the horse thirsty.

Remember that not every time an order is not signed does it mean you missed a sale. Not necessarily. Actually, if you're doing your job, a sale is not made during every visit or contact.

Let's say you have done an excellent job of motivating your likely buyer. You talked a great deal about the benefits of the purchase. You probed and listened. You did everything right.

You stop. You ask for the order. The person says, "Not now, maybe later."

That's not necessarily a *no*. Keep in regular contact. Even if it's not to ask for the order. If you do a good job of remaining in contact and cultivating, sooner or later (hopefully sooner rather than later!) they will buy.

Tepid. At this level, you may or may not make the sale—no matter how ardent your attempt to persuade them. I find that quite early in your presentation, you'll spot these people. But don't give up. Your enthusiasm and persistence may pay off.

Keep in mind people buy things for their reasons. Not yours.

You cannot manipulate a person into buying. That's not integrity selling. It won't work. And it's not right.

The only way to get a person to buy something is by making the person want to do it. There is no other way.

Your job is to help them recognize how valuable your product is to them. They won't buy it just because you want them to.

Cold. This is the Inert Fifth. They will not make a purchase, no matter how brilliant your presentation. You performed a perfect *gargouillade* (one of ballet's most difficult movements where the dancer makes a mighty leap in the air and simulates wide circles with their feet).

It doesn't matter. They still won't buy!

You don't need my book on *Supremely Successful Selling* to know early in your time with this last group that you've struck a dry well. Take your leave. You have others to call on. Thank them for the visit and wish them well. Bless and release.

You will find you are far more productive if you spend more time and energy on the first three levels. That will pay the greatest dividends for you and give you the most satisfaction.

I'll work with the fourth group (Tepid). But not much. I'll have a better reading on them after a few visits—and may end up putting them in the fifth level.

And those Inert Fifth, after a visit, two at the most—avoid them.

Here is the important lesson. Remember—I asked you to make this your sales creed. In order to ensure your success and production, spend 85 percent of your time on the top three levels, 10 percent on the fourth level, and 5 percent on the fifth.

I am telling Egizio Bianchini about my five levels. He is the global head for the giant BMO Bankcorp. I ask him if the levels are the same for selling something like banking and investments.

"Absolutely," he tells me. "Our sales group spends virtually no time on the latter two groups. It's not worth it. A waste of time and energy."

I then ask him what sets his bank apart. What makes it one of the leaders in the world? Why are its salespeople among the most highly regarded in the field?

"I can tell you what it is. We don't sell banking. And we don't sell investments. We sell ideas. And because our customers know our ethics, they never question our motives."

That's selling with integrity!

7 | It's a Numbers Game

GET READY. Get set. You're ready to begin.

You will find one of the most difficult steps in making the sale is actually not the face-to-face presentation. And it's not the heart-beats-faster moment when you actually ask for the order.

What's most difficult is getting in front of the buyer. Face to face.

Ah, that's the tough part. It takes steely determination and persistence, unyielding resolve. Difficult situations do not build character. They reveal it. You feel like Sisyphus—you keep pushing that boulder up the steep hill.

But, I've discovered a great truth. If you find a path with no obstacles, it probably doesn't lead anywhere.

Here's the good news. When you get the face-to-face, you are *85 percent* on your way to making the sale. All of our studies indicate this. This is true whether it's in an office, a home, or over the counter.

But here's the rub. Getting the visit is harder than making the sale.

Note, I don't call this an *appointment* if you are arranging to see someone in their home or office. That may seem like a small matter, not calling it an appointment. But as we know in this business of sales, success is in the details. Inch perfect.

The word *appointment* has a negative connotation. If you need to have a root canal, you call your dentist for an appointment. Or to see a proctologist, you call for an appointment. (Not for the same problem!)

But a *visit*, that's quite different, quite pleasant. I call it, the persistent and joyful pursuit of the sale.

The call you make for a visit is the first step in the rewarding and jubilant journey. You're giving your likely buyers an opportunity to invest in something that will enrich their lives.

Bring great pleasure and satisfaction. What could be more rewarding for you than that? Edmund Wilson calls it, "a blaze of heartfelt ecstasy."

Here's what I do. If it's a cold call, I always send a letter in advance of phoning for a visit. I've worried about sending the letter ahead of the call. I worried whether the letter would actually prompt some turndowns or make it impossible to get through on the phone. Does it give the person extra time to prepare arguments for declining a visit?

I can assure you that sending a letter is the most effective way possible of securing the visit. And on top of everything else, it does save 5 or 10 minutes in trying to explain on the phone why you want to see the person.

I'm going to give you a sample letter you can use as a guide. It will be most effective if you tweak it to sound more like you. It's in the appendix of the book. By the way, you send it as a hard copy on attractive stationery, not an e-mail.

In the chapter you just finished, I suggested that you should ask those who fall in the two highest levels of buying if you can use their names in making other contacts or use them as references. In your letter, be certain to include the name of the person who gave you the reference and suggested you call. It will help clinch the visit.

Add something like this to your letter: "Your friends, Tommy and Terry Johnson, suggested I write to ask for some time with you. I believe you will be as interested in our discussion as they were." Or something of the sort.

Note that in the letter, you are very clear you won't be asking them to buy something. No—not on this visit!

There are two reasons for this. First of all, I find that by assuring the person the visit is entirely exploratory and interpretive, you're much more likely to get to see him or her.

And second, it's a good technique since it's almost certain you're going to need two visits to make the sale if it's for a large amount or a stop-and-think decision.

How many calls do you have to make to get the visit?

If it's cold calls, I find that for every 10 attempts, I reach 4 first-time buyers. Of the four, two will turn out to be people who will see me. Of the people who will see me, one out of three will buy.

That means that in order to make a sale, you need to be in direct contact with three people. That means 30 cold calls. That's hard work. No one said it would be easy.

Just remember—don't let anyone outwork you. You are what you repeatedly do. Success then is not a lucky act. It is a habit. Luck is preparation and persistence meeting opportunity.

That's what it takes and it's tough. You will be experiencing what the Russians call *vyshaya mera*—"the highest form of pain and punishment." I keep remembering that a diamond is a chunk of coal that made good under pressure.

"In a way," Dortch Oldham tells me, "it's a numbers game. If you make enough calls and contacts, you'll make your sales objective. It's that simple. Make those calls.

"I tell my people that when they're ready to wrap it up for the day—don't quit. Make one more call. The difference between an adequate salesperson and a really successful one is most often just making one more call."

Even with ordinary talent, if it is combined with extraordinary and unflinching perseverance, all things are possible. But it takes having an objective. That's essential.

It's a numbers game. Be realistic, but set the bar high so you have to stand on tiptoes to reach it.

Write down your objective. That's essential. Put it down on paper. Think about it as you write it down. Program it into your subconscious and it will take on a power all its own. Give yourself deadlines—objectives for the month, the week, and each day.

Aim high. Aim higher. Aim higher still. A salesperson without a definite objective is like a ship without a rudder—stalled and adrift.

Persistence does pay off. Determination ignites the human spirit. It is the engine that propels salespeople to greatness.

Mary Ellen Rodgers worked for five years (five years!) cultivating a huge potential client—calling, cultivating, simply showing up. The client had been using another firm for 40 years, but Mary Ellen finally won them over.

"It was more than just expertise," Mary Ellen tells me. "That's expected. It was new ideas and what we could bring to them. It turns out now to be one of our largest accounts.

"Persistence and hard work is the key to success. You need to remember that success in sales is a marathon not a sprint," she points out.

The question you face is: "Am I willing to do whatever it takes to get what I want and be successful?" You are the hero of your own story.

Just try one more time—that's my credo. I like what I'm about to tell you regarding the importance of tenacity and persistence.

Marc Connelly wrote a wonderful play entitled *The Green Pastures*. It is a colloquial story about God's persistence. There's one scene that's particularly memorable.

The Lord and Gabriel were having a serious discussion on man's sorry record in building a better world. The Lord has tried everything to dissuade mankind from its sins and foolish actions. Gabriel is about to blow his trumpet and put an end to it all.

Just as Gabriel lifts his trumpet to his lips, the Lord says: "Hold it, Gabe. I'm gonna try one more time."

8

Failing to Prepare Is Preparing to Fail

SETTING THE VISIT can be tough. I know how dif

I've been selling for a long time. I find I agonize more about making the phone call for the visit than I do about the actual presentation to the likely buyer.

So don't be concerned if you feel pangs of anxiety. I've found that without challenge, there is no achievement. Remember, when you get the visit you're 85 percent on your way to making the sale.

Here are 13 steps that are necessary to ease those palpitations in the tummy and help ensure that you get to see the person. George Allen, the renowned football coach, says that winning can be defined as the science of being totally prepared. Luck doesn't favor the lucky. It favors the prepared.

1. Send the type of letter I've recommended. There's a sample in the appendix. Be certain to revise it in any way that helps make it your own.

2. Practice (practice, practice) your opening. Even with all my years, I still write out what I am going to say on the phone. Success happens when luck meets preparation and practice.

   A reporter interviewed history's greatest cellist, Pablo Cassals, on his 90th birthday. "Why are you still practicing four hours a day after all these years?" he asked Cassals.

   "Because I think I am making progress."

3. Even though I prepare a script, so to speak, I, of course, don't read it. It has to sound spontaneous.

   Writing it out means I don't miss anything. And the truth is, it gives me confidence. Keep in mind Winston Churchill's admonition: "I have to practice a great deal in order to make a speech sound spontaneous."

4. Have a calendar handy. Remember, your purpose in making the call is to set the date for the visit. Get ready.

5. This is probably the most difficult part of all. You know you have to make the call for the visit. You face the phone with dread and fear. You begin reciting the war chant of the Turkish army calvary: *Today, die with honor.*

I know how you feel. I've been there myself. Remember—the difficulties in life are intended to make us better, not bitter.

You stare at the phone. Minutes go by. You know that at some point, you have to punch in the numbers. But you hope the phone will ring, so you won't have to make the dreaded call. But the telephone doesn't ring.

You're feeling like Lance Armstrong who sent his family a text message after his first Tour de France. "Oh my God. Ouch. Terrible. Unbelievably painful."

Resolve that you'll fling the whole weight of your spirit into it. Okay, get ready. But wait. There's one thing I'm going to suggest that I know will help you.

6. Stand up. If you don't believe this helps, just try it. Standing releases a flow of energy that simply doesn't exist when you're sitting. Best of all, I actually like a wireless phone so I can do some pacing.

You know what? When I stand, I feel I can lick the world. I can make that call. I'll get that visit. I'm standing and I'm determined. You'll feel exactly the same. Life is good.

7. Smile when you talk. Your likely buyer will "hear" the smile in your voice. Explain that you're following up on the letter you sent. You want to know when it might be convenient to meet.

Be resoundingly positive. If you expect the worst, you'll never be disappointed.

8. Keep the small talk brief. No chit-chat. Oh, certainly be cordial and pleasant. But your focus has to be on setting the visit.

"Hi, Mary. This is Jerry Panas. I sent you a letter the other day about something I believe will be very important in your life. It's about our new product. You remember, your friend Ken B. Easy suggested I call you. When is a good time to see you and Tommy—next Tuesday or Thursday?"

That may strike you as terse. Okay, do what's comfortable. But your task is not to engage in extended conversation. Your job is to get the visit.

9. Be up front about the amount of time you'll need. *"I'd like an hour with you. Will that be all right?"*

What happens if the likely buyer tells you she can only give you 20 minutes?

"Well, I was hoping for more time, but if your schedule is tight, let's do it in 20 minutes. I think this is so important I'm willing to take whatever time you've got." (You have probably found, as I have, that when a person tells you she can only give you 15 or 20 minutes, she ends up giving you all the time you need.)

10. Be focused. On the telephone call, your job is to set the date for the visit. It's not to make the sale or discuss the product. Don't fall into the trap of trying to make the sale on the phone. It won't work. (This doesn't apply to a telemarketer.)

There are some minefields to avoid. *"Send some material. I'll look it over and be back to you."* Or, *"Tell me more over the phone."* Consider comments like these as treason to the cause.

Be prepared. Keep in mind that when an objection is made, the discussion is just beginning.

Your mission is to get the visit. You must have optimism, faith, quiet determination, and a spirited attitude. If you take the right road and keep at it—sometime, somewhere, you will come out at the right place.

11. Move the conversation on and set the date. I like giving a person a choice of dates: *"What's best for you, Terry, next Tuesday or next Thursday."* Social psychologists tell us that a person is much more apt to make a positive decision if there is a choice.

12. In the appendix, I give you a roster of objections. I've tested these. I don't believe you can add one that isn't on the list.

   Study the objections. Be prepared to answer all of them. You're bound to get at least one. Don't say I didn't warn you. In selling, it's not whether you get knocked down—it's whether you get up.

13. Great! You got the date. You're well on your way to making the sale. Follow the phone call immediately with a letter of confirmation and appreciation. Make it brief (Letter 2 in the appendix).

   I never call to confirm a date before the visit. In fact, I try to make myself virtually unreachable! I don't want to make it convenient or easy for a person to cancel at the last minute. I let my letter put all the arrangements in place.

   Aim for some early successes. First, call the likely buyers you feel are the easiest to talk with.

   Secure the visit. After a few calls, you will have the model down pat.

   Your success will depend on getting the visit. If they are willing to see you, you're 85 percent on your way to making the sale.

   Securing the visit is your overriding objective. It will be the result of your resolve and a winning attitude.

Let me tell you about the shoe salesman whose territory was in a remote part of Africa. After a week, he e-mailed his boss at the company.

"Bring me back. You can't sell shoes here. Everyone goes around barefoot."

They brought him home and sent another salesman. After a week or so, the new salesman e-mailed the company.

"This is a wonderful territory. It's a great opportunity for the company. There's enormous potential. No one has shoes."

Melanie Sabelhaus says a positive attitude is essential. "I want my salespeople to be self-motivated. I want them to have fire in their bellies."

9

Go the Extra Mile that Failures Refuse to Travel

LET ME SET THE SCENE. Everyone will benefit from this chapter. But if you're in the type of selling where you have to get an appointment, this chapter is especially for you.

You are about to make the phone call to get the visit. You know that if you get to see the likely buyer, you are well on your way to making the sale.

Here's what I want you to do. Put yourself in the buyer's shoes. Think like the buyer. Become the buyer.

Look at it from the buyer's viewpoint. In Chicago's Millenium Park, they have some tables permanently set with a chessboard marking.

I stop to watch two old-timers intent on their chess game. It is obvious these are experienced old pros. The match is well under way. One of the men gets up. He stands behind his opponent.

He wants to look at the board from the opponent's side of the table. He seeks a different perspective. He wants to think like his opponent.

That's what I want you to do. In making the call for the visit, I want you to look at it from the likely buyer's side of the table. Look at the situation from his perspective.

You're ready to make the phone call for the visit. Stand!

You dial the number. The likely buyer is on the phone. You've gone through the initial pleasantries. You have your calendar handy.

The moment has come. If you are uneasy about making these calls, or even a bit timid, I can identify with that.

After all these years, I still feel the same anxiety. There is no pleasure in these calls. I look upon them as an occasion for spiritual testing!

But you know you must make the call. Your purpose is to set the date.

Remember, the people you call want to know, "Can he really help me? Can I trust him? Why should I listen to him? What's in it for me?"

Get ready.

"John. I want to bring you news about something you are going to find important in your business. I think it will save you time and money. As you saw from my letter, Ken B. Easy suggested I call you. I believe you will find it as important and useful in your business as he did. Is Tuesday or Wednesday of next week the better day for us to get together?"

I wish it was easy, but often it's not. The one thing you can expect—is the unexpected. Sometimes you run into a problem. Every winner has scars.

Someone asked Frank Shorter, the great marathoner, what pleasure he took in running for so many years. "Pleasure?" he said. "I don't understand the question. I don't take any pleasure in it. I do it for the pain."

"Jerry, I'm not sure it's a good idea to get together. I don't believe I'm interested in buying and I'm terribly busy now. It wouldn't be a good use of my time or yours."

You hoped for better—but didn't get it. You could leave it at that, thank the person for his consideration, and go on to the next person on your list. But you know better. The secrets of success don't work unless you do.

You understand it's going to take a personal visit to make the sale. You are also certain that if he would only meet with you, he would become engaged and interested. You have to exert yourself. This isn't easy. You'd prefer having your teeth scraped, but you go on.

"I think this is something you're going to find important, John. The choice to meet is entirely yours. I'm not smart enough to persuade you to do something you don't want to do. But I feel so strongly this is something you will find interesting that I'm going to press just a little bit. (Tell him "Ken was certain"—if you're using Ken as a reference.) *I am so certain this is something you will find attractive that I'm going to ask again if we can visit. But you know me well enough* (if it's someone you have met) *to know you can be honest and I'll respect whatever you decide. What day is better for you next week, Tuesday or Wednesday?"*

There, you did it. You made the call. It wasn't easy, but you did it.

"Jerry, just tell me what you're looking for. Maybe we can do this on the phone. I really don't have much time. And frankly, I'm not crazy about being called on."

This isn't getting any easier. What's the old Chinese torture—having your toenails pulled? I think I'd prefer that. But I won't give up. Not yet.

"I just don't feel comfortable trying to handle this on the phone. It's too important. Look, I'm willing to give it a few minutes if you can give me that much time, too. Will you do that for me? Will you give me a few minutes? What's going to be better for you, Tuesday or Wednesday? We can cover this quickly. I'm convinced this is going to be important to you. It will save you time and money."

What happens if you're still swimming upstream and the current is against you? Your person says:

"Look, why don't you just e-mail me all of the information. I'll look it over and I'll make a decision."

You know that would be the worst of options. If you come to an obstacle, turn it into an opportunity. Take one more shot.

"I really believe you would give it a careful reading. But, the material simply can't convey the importance and excitement of this product. I really believe it's something that will interest you and save you money. I know how busy you are, but I'm willing to take as little time as you can give me. When can I come to see you? Next Tuesday or Wednesday?"

Every time I call for a visit, I think of a couple of lines from *Waiting for Godot*. They keep running through my mind. Estragon says: "I can't go on like this." Vladimir replies: "That's what you think."

These are just a few of the stiff-arms you can get from someone you call. They're legitimate. I don't even call them objections. They're the kind of responses you should expect. If you incur stumbling blocks, use them as stepping-stones. Keep climbing.

Remember, your job is to get the visit. It's not to make the case or try to sell the product on the phone or send an e-mail, as much as your likely buyer may try to corner you into doing so.

You don't want to be rude and you certainly don't want him to hang up on you. But you know that a personal visit greatly increases your opportunity for a sale. Remember, success is simply having a good product plus persistence.

"Listen, Jerry, why don't you tell me what this is all about. We could probably do a lot of this on the phone. Tell me about the product."

"It's a great product, John. The truth is, I couldn't do it justice on the phone or by e-mail. I have a feeling this is something you're going to be interested in, and I have some photographs and material I want to share with you. You're going to find this important. When is a good time to meet you next week, Tuesday or Wednesday?"

I want to caution you not to solicit on the telephone—as much as he may try to move you in that direction.

"We're both so busy, Jerry. I know you're coming to talk with me about buying something but I think we can handle this on the phone—and save some time. Just tell me about it now?

"I'm certain this is something that's going to interest you, John, and that's why I'm so keen on seeing you. I don't feel I can do it justice on the phone. I think we'd both lose if I tried.

"I know how busy you are. The folks I'm calling on are all terribly busy. That's why I'm careful about the time I take for a visit. I'm sure we can wrap this all up in a few minutes. I'm hoping you'll give me that much time.

"I'm not smart enough to talk you into buying something you don't want or isn't good for you. But I do want to see you. When is a good day for a visit next week, Tuesday or Wednesday?"

I have one more suggestion. It gets wonderful results. You can count on it. It almost always turns the person around. Use it only as your last resort.

"I know how busy you are, John. That's one of the reasons I'm eager to see you. You're the kind of person who gets things done and makes decisions.

"I hate the feeling that I'm pressuring you. I hope you don't take it that way. But if I didn't ask just once more, we both would be losing an important opportunity. I'm so excited about this product I just feel I must see you.

"I'll take whatever time you give me. No sales pitch. I promise. When's a good time to see you, next Tuesday or Wednesday. If I take more than 10 minutes, I'll give you my watch!"

Try it. You're going to find this works.

Here's an important tip. Practice my responses. Repeat them over and over. But make them your own. Use words and sentences the way you would say them. As the Welsh proverb has it, you must sing with the voice God gave you.

And be certain to review The Objections to Getting the Visit in the appendix (I referred to this in the last chapter). Practice your responses until they flow.

I can promise you something. If you make enough calls, you will acquire what the Germans refer to as *Fingerspitzen Gefühl*—a certain comfort and instinct that leads to success.

Here's the good news. If you make your calls, you will get your visits. Be persistent. Successful salespeople are simply ordinary people with extraordinary determination.

The word "begin" is full of vitality and power. The only way to get something done is to begin. Just begin. You're never finished if you forever keep beginning.

The miracle isn't that you finished the call and got to see the buyer. The miracle is that you had the determination and courage to start. History will record you are an Olympian.

10 | Sometimes You Have to Be Silent to Be Heard

DO YOU FEEL the same way I do?

I really enjoy shopping for a car. I like hearing about all the good stuff—the carburetor, the compression ratio, the manifold. I even ask about the length of the axle.

I don't know a darn thing about what any of that means. I just think I'm supposed to ask those questions to appear auto-savvy.

What I really like is to wallow in the leather seats. I like an instrument panel that looks like the cockpit of a 747. I also like to see how the various salespeople in the showroom handle themselves.

Well, Felicity and I were shopping for a new car recently. We walk into the showroom. We begin looking at one of the first cars in our path.

Before I can even turn around, a salesman comes up to me. He sticks out his hand, introduces himself, and begins singing the virtues of the car we are glancing at. We have a tedious discourse on gas consumption, safety features, and motor efficiency.

Here's what I found interesting. Not once does he take time to ask us any questions. Not a single question. He would have put a televangelist to shame.

He has absolutely no idea what we might be interested in. Some folks aren't hard of hearing. They're hard of listening.

He should have followed the advice of Zig Ziglar, the *über* master of salesmanship: You can sell anything you want if you will just understand what the other person wants. No one ever listens himself out of a sale.

We escape from that place as soon as possible. We move on to another auto dealer not far away.

We are greeted at the door by a salesperson. She spends the first 15 or 20 minutes peppering us with questions. She wants to know about our needs, the size of the family, what we have in mind, the amount and type of traveling we do, and whether this would be our primary car or a second car.

By the time she finishes, she seems to know precisely the car we want. No surprise! She passes several cars in the showroom, then takes us to the car she feels best meets our needs. We end up buying it.

Now let me tell you about her superb follow-through.

We drive the car home. The next day, we get a telephone call from the salesperson. She just wants to make certain everything is working properly and we are happy. She says if there are any problems at all, we are to call her.

There's more. A week later, I receive a call from the dealer's head of repair and maintenance. He just wants me to know that if there is ever any problem at all, they will bring a loaner, a new car, to the house and pick up my car and service it. He assures me, however, that is very unlikely. "These cars go on forever."

Richard O'Donnell has the Buick dealership in San Gabriel, California. For years, his auto agency has been number one in sales in the country for Buick. Number one in the country!

Dick tells his salespeople not to begin by selling cars. "In fact, if you do it right you don't sell at all. You find out everything you possibly can about the buyer. Then show them the car they should have. They're sold."

Most probable buyers won't really listen or pay attention to what you are trying to sell until they're absolutely convinced you've heard and appreciated their point of view. As Montaigne said, what a person wants most in life is to be heard.

People buy your product for their reasons, not yours. You cannot manipulate or maneuver a person into buying. No matter how much mumbo-jumbo you feed them, you won't make the sale.

You sell with integrity. That's foremost. It's not selling what you want to sell. It's selling what the buyer wants to buy.

You motivate, arouse their interest, and help them recognize the value of your product. But they won't buy just because you want them to.

Bonnie McElveen Hunter tells me she considers listening one of the most important factors in selling. "If you don't listen carefully, how will you know what the buyer needs, wants most, and is willing to pay?" I am going to give you the grave mistakes you make in selling if you don't listen effectively. Note them well. They make the difference between success and failure.

If you don't listen:

1. You don't learn anything about the likely buyer. You will never know his needs and desires. If you do all the talking, it's all about you.
2. You won't hear any concerns she might have because you're not probing.
3. You won't uncover any buying-clues. You won't discover the buyer's motivation. You won't be able to claim, clutch, and capture the buyer's intent.
4. Your likely buyer is more apt to buy when he's talking than when you're talking.
5. You won't understand what she's willing to invest in.
6. You never have to regret what you don't say. Light travels faster than sound. That is why some salespeople seem bright until you hear them speak.
7. If you're doing all the talking, you provide more opportunity for him to disagree with you on some of your statements.

   Craftsmen who do woodworking talk about "working with the grain." What they mean is that smoothing a surface requires working with the fibers of the wood and not against them. By listening, you're working with the grain.

8. You dominate the conversation instead of guiding it. Sometimes silence is the very best answer.
9. The spotlight is on you instead of the likely buyer. You need to give her center stage.
10. You don't give yourself breathing time to think ahead.

Here comes your most important lesson. You don't have to ask for the order. You *listen* the sale. Yes, just listen.

You've heard about salespeople who talk too much. But you have never heard about a salesman who listens too much.

Note this well. In order to *listen the sale*, you talk during the presentation for 25 percent of the time. The likely buyer talks for the balance, 75 percent of the time.

It's the most effective way to be on the same wavelength with the person and make him feel you have really listened. It becomes his agenda, not yours.

That's *supremely successful selling, and with integrity.*

Reader, do we see things the same way? It would be nice to get together and compare notes to make absolutely certain, but I think we do. Make it a give-and-take process. But as far as you're concerned, it's mostly take. I'm convinced that effective salespeople don't really sell. They listen the sale.

You ask and probe so you can act inside the mind and heart of the buyer. Keep in mind that the person actually in charge of the conversation is the salesperson asking questions and probing.

Think of the attorney who is exploring, investigating, and asking the witness relevant questions. It's the attorney who is in charge.

That's why I call these sessions with the likely buyer *innerviews,* not interviews. Do you see the distinction? By explorative listening in the *innerview,* you get inside a person.

Here's a lesson I've learned. I listen as if I am hard of hearing. And I listen with my eyes.

There's something else I know. Good listeners are not only popular, but after awhile they learn something.

If you listen carefully enough, you'll know precisely his needs and greatest passions. You'll learn what to ask for and what will motivate the person to make the purchase.

Here's the clue as to why listening ensures the sale.

In your first meeting, 55 percent of the buyer's perception of you is based on your appearance. That's why they say you don't have a second opportunity to make a first impression.

There's more—38 percent of the impression is based on your voice. And only 7 percent on what you actually say. Good grief—only 7 percent.

But it gets worse.

After 48 hours, they remember 78 percent of what they say. And only 34 percent of what you say.

That's why it's so essential you listen. You probe, you question, you listen.

I got these statistics one day from Norman Augustine. At the time he was CEO of Lockheed Martin. He had commissioned a study and these were the results.

In selling with integrity, listening makes it possible to understand the buyer's needs. It increases the trust, confidence, and respect for the seller. Listening builds a personal relationship and bonding.

Listening is the salesperson's scripture. You listen the sale.

11

Be Like the Busy Spider

I WAS REMEMBERING MARY KAY ASH the other day. That magical woman founded an empire because she simply didn't know it couldn't be done.

It reminded me that things aren't always what they seem. It made me think of the grade school children lined up in the school cafeteria one day. At the head of the table is a large pile of apples.

One of the teachers made a note. She posted it by the apple tray. "Take only one apple. God is watching."

Moving further down the line, at the other end of the table, is a large pile of delicious looking chocolate cookies. A child had written a note: "Take all you want. God is watching the apples."

Life is full of surprises. That's why I thought of that story.

Back to Mary Kay Ash. I'm having lunch with her. I am involved with her in an important project in Dallas.

We are finishing dessert. I am talking with her about what I think is a more effective training of her 1,000-plus salespeople for selling cosmetics.

That gentle woman has a way of looking at you when she is upset that would send birds scurrying from the trees. "Jerry, at Mary Kay we don't sell cosmetics."

"You don't?" I ask—a bit taken aback.

"No. We sell hope."

The statement is actually attributed to Charles Revson (founder of Revlon). But who cares! When you're sitting across the luncheon table from Mary Kay and she says it—it comes alive.

It's not your dramatic presentation that makes the sale, sad to say. Even if you finish with a grandstand flourish and a daring double backward somersault—that won't make the sale.

And it's not your fancy material that makes the sale. Save that for a follow-up visit. Use it to give more detail about your product and its portentous value.

What, then, are the important factors in motivating the buyer? It's actually not entirely about your product—although that, of course, weighs heavily. And it's certainly not about you.

It's all about your likely buyer. You need to connect the dots. If you have probed and listened carefully (75 percent of the session), you will know precisely what she will buy and what motivates her.

Above all else, know your buyer. You must have a carefully grounded understanding of the buyer's needs and wants. The art of selling with integrity soon teaches you that people buy for their reasons, not yours.

Now put that together and sell the magic. The good news is that it doesn't have to be a blinding presentation, sparkled with glitter and fire. Not many are capable of that. I'm not.

You must know your buyer. You must know the motivating buttons to push. You sell the dream. Sell the magic.

I have what I call a salesman's credo. You make the sale before you ask for the order.

Let me see if I can make this a little clearer. When a person goes into a hardware store to buy a drill, he doesn't go to the hardware store because he needs a drill. He buys a drill because he needs a hole.

See what I mean? If you're selling the drill, you're not selling the magic.

I also learned in our studies that your printed material is not important. I'm reminded that the shelf life of the average four-color brochure of your product is somewhere between milk and yogurt.

Oh, certainly, you need material. But don't be waving it around or pulling it out immediately. You'll break the spell.

Your likely buyer will be much more attentive to your oral presentation. Convey the magic. Romance the hole, not the drill.

In studies we've conducted, it is always the oral presentation that motivates the sale. In fact, most buyers can't remember the printed material.

Am I rigid about this—that the material is not important? Of course not. Remember, selling is more an art than a science.

I worked with Tommy Shores, one of the most effective salesmen I know. One look at Tommy's beautiful brochure would capture the heart of any homemaker.

When I coached his sales staff, I admonished them to first know the buyers. If you don't, they may love the furniture in the brochure but still not buy. That's because you tried to move them from the brochure to the pocketbook instead of from the heart to the pocketbook.

"It's not just the quality of furniture," Tommy told me once. "We need to get inside the minds and souls of our buyers. I try to take them by the hand and walk them into their homes and into the rooms where my furniture will sit. I want it to be a love affair.

"I tell my salespeople not to sell the features. Oh sure, the customer needs to know that much of our furniture is fashioned by hand, not machine. And we talk about the quality of the leather, the best in the marketplace—and how we wash it down by hand three times before we dye it."

"But what really sells the piece," Tommy tells me, "is that I have the buyer visualize where the couch is going in the room, how it will look, and how much the family will enjoy it."

Buck Rogers (yes, Buck is his real name!) was the greatest salesman in the history of Big Blue. He rose in the company to become senior vice president of IBM.

"What makes the difference?" I asked him once. "What do you tell your salespeople?"

"It's very simple," he said. "I tell them that at IBM, we don't sell equipment. We sell solutions."

Typically when I sell, I don't bring out the brochures until the very end. There are times when I don't even do that.

Consider carefully the three qualities of your product. They are: features, functions, and benefits. It is important to make a distinction in your selling.

A feature of your product is an explanation of what it does. How it performs. The number of copies per minute your copy machine can produce, or the number of stitches per inch, or the car's acceleration from 0 to 60 in 7 seconds. Those are features.

When I think of function, I conjure up some particular part of the product. For instance, the radio works on AC or batteries. Your cell phone does everything—including take photos. Your watch glows in the dark. Those are all functions. It is a part of your product.

But a benefit—ah, that's the real advantage in using your product. That's the sizzle. The *snap, crackle, pop.*

It is what your product will do for the probable buyer that sells.

Arthur Brown & Co., in New York, is one of the largest sellers of fountain pens in the country. Adrienne Bayuk is in charge of the sales force. She estimates, by the way, that there are 5 to 6 million people (mostly men) who use or collect fountain pens. (Divide that in half and that's still a lot of people.)

The other day, she was talking to me about the virtues of the German Pelikan pen. This proved to be a good example of features, functions, and benefits.

The Pelikan fountain pen has a large ink capacity. And an 18-karat gold nib. Those are features.

The clip is shaped like a pelican's beak. That's fetching, but the clip is a function. It holds the pen to your pocket.

But the fact that the Pelikan has the smoothest writing nib ever developed and has a perfect flow of ink — that's the benefit. "It writes like magic," she tells me. (I bought the pen.)

The benefit deals with what your product will do for the buyer. It rises like a wave and you ride it to the finish.

Don't sell the features or the functions. Buyers are drawn to the magic of an idea. Sell the benefits. Sell the magic. Sell like a busy spider, spinning the web, until it eventually captivates and captures the buyer.

12

Amazing What You Can Do When You Don't Know What You Can't Do

YOU HAVE TAKEN the important first step. You sent the letter to set up the visit.

Next, you made the phone call. You established the date. In some ways, it really wasn't as difficult as you thought it would be—even though the phone call didn't follow your script exactly. It never does.

You're now 85 percent on your way to making the sale. I remind you that it's harder to get the visit than it is to make the sale. That's one of the important truths of selling.

Then, faster than you expected, the day arrives and you're in the home or office of your buyer. It's what Vladimir Nabokov called, "moments of happiness, of rapture, when your soul is laid bare."

The first order of business, of course, is to establish a rapport and common ground. You need to get to know your buyer. This is not a time for social chitchat. The main thing is to keep the main thing the main thing.

You probe. You ask questions. You find out as much as you can about the needs and desires of the buyer. The archer strikes the target—partly by pulling, partly by letting go.

There's no magic to how long this should take. Take whatever time is necessary. Just be sure that small talk doesn't dominate your session and steal from your clear mission. Your objective is to make the sale.

During the innerview, you learn everything possible about the buyer. You get inside his mind and the deepest reaches of his heart.

No matter how winsome you are, your buyer knows you're not there on a social call or an inquiry about his health. He's thinking: "When is she going to ask me to buy?" Or, "How much is this going to cost?" Or, "I wonder where she got my name?" Or, "Why the devil did I agree to this visit?"

That's what's going through the buyer's head. He's not hearing a word you're saying. I know it's true. I've learned this in study after study we've conducted.

Here's what I suggest. I want you to try it. You needn't use my words. Find your own rhythm and what works best for you and turns your words into music. The Talmud teaches that you should use only the voice God has given you.

A good bit of the selling I do is in the nonprofit world. I am involved in soliciting gifts. Some might say that's the most difficult thing possible to sell—intangibles. Selling widgets is far easier. Not true! Not if you're selling something you really believe in.

I called on Jim recently. He loves his university and went there on a scholarship. I begin my visit this way.

"I've come today, Jim, to talk with you about the university and its vision for the future. There's a project in particular I want to discuss—it's something I think you'll be interested in. (Pause.) I'm not going to ask you for a gift today. I want to make that clear. We're not even going to discuss money. I just want to tell you about this project. But I'll be coming back and when I do, I'm going to ask you for a great deal of money. But not today."

Being clear at the outset that you're not going to try to sell on this visit overcomes immense emotional blocks and hurdles. I've put Jim's mind at ease.

Jim actually begins listening to me then. He takes his hands out of his pockets. He no longer clutches his wallet.

As I talk about the program, I discover that Jim is finding part of the presentation irresistible. (Remember my admonition: Sell the dream.) I can tell. It is burning inside his heart and mind.

I ask open questions: "Jim, how do you feel about this program?" I probe. I listen. I test for concerns. I'm not ready yet to ask. Remember, when eating an elephant take one bite at a time.

We have a thorough discussion. Up to this point, I still haven't shown him any material. A good salesperson explains. A better salesperson demonstrates. The best salesperson inspires.

I give Jim plenty of opportunity to ask his own questions. We're getting near the end of the visit. Finally I get to that point where I'd normally ask for a gift (or in the case of discussing a product, try to make the sale). Instead, I do something pretty much like this with Jim. (Remember, I told him I wasn't going to ask for a gift on this call.)

"It's been wonderful having the time with you. And I can see you're interested in the program. I was certain you would be. Pull out your calendar. I want to set a time for another visit."

Almost always, the person will say: *"Aw, come on—there's no need to set another date. We can talk about the money today. It's okay. I know you have something in mind."* That's almost exactly what Jim did say. Ah, you have lanced the boil.

Here's my response:

"The truth is, Jim, I'm not smart enough to know how much you should give. That's really your decision. But for a program like this, I feel you would want to make a gift of $1 million."

Note, I don't say he *should* make a gift of $1 million. I say I am pretty sure he would *want* to make a gift of that size. Note my words. I choose them carefully.

"I thought you would want . . . ."

I haven't even asked for a gift. I've merely mentioned what I feel Jim would want to do for a program of this importance and interest to him. The world is round and what may seem like almost the beginning may be the end.

We negotiate and talk some more. He raises some valid concerns. In the end, it does take another visit—but I know I am well on my way to getting the gift. And I did! If at first you do succeed, try to hide your astonishment.

The Finnish have a word for what you've just achieved: *sisu*. It's finding within yourself that extra ingredient that results in you accomplishing something very special and extraordinary.

Here's something important to keep in mind no matter what you're selling. You can't leave without getting a commitment to something—a sale or a new date for another meeting.

Follow these directions and you are headed for deep-water success and greatness. I promise.

Flourishing achievement in selling requires tenacity and hard work. Bill Bradley, the Hall of Fame basketball player and former U.S. senator, said: "I might lose because I wasn't tall enough. I might lose because I wasn't fast enough. But I'm not going to lose because I didn't work hard enough."

Take a lesson from St. Paul's message to the people of Corinth (Corinthians 9:24). "You do know that all who run in the race, do indeed run. But only one receives the prize. So run hard to win."

Work hard to win. It means you must drive to win, to get things done. Cultivate the urge to compete. Be determined.

I love the comment my friend Rich DeVos gave me: "If I had to name one characteristic I believe is most important in sales, I would say it's persistence. Determination. It's the will to endure to the end. To get knocked down 70 times, then get up off the floor saying: Okay. Great! Here comes 71."

It's the pride and passion to win. A can-do attitude. You do these things. You become the successful salesperson you are meant to be.

13 | Listen! I Think I Hear a Sale

I FIND MY EARLY FEW MINUTES with a likely buyer are often my most valuable. I don't engage in idle chatter. I'm actually on a fact-finding mission.

I probe. I ask questions. Mostly, I listen. The more you listen, the smarter you get.

After I spend time getting to know the likely buyer much better, I begin asking questions about our product. Are you surprised I'm not touting my product. You're right. I want the buyer to talk and promote it. Here are some questions I ask.

- Tell me a little bit about what you might know about our products. How did you hear about us?
- If you know about us, tell me what you think of our product.
- How do you see yourself and your family using our product?
- You have been using a product similar to ours. What would you like to change most to make it the most valuable to you?

You will note these are all open-ended questions. You really haven't spent a lot of time talking about your product. Not yet! But you're discovering important selling clues.

You don't listen to respond. You listen to gain information. That's a very important distinction.

While you're uncovering valuable information, you're gaining rapport. You will find that the more time you take in securing a bond, the less it will appear later that you're using pressure.

That's what I mean by selling with integrity. You motivate. You do not pressure.

If you're talking, let's say, to a corporate purchasing agent and you're not quite sure how great his interest is (and often this will be the case)—you need to fully explore the situation.

"We've talked a good bit about your company and what you feel your greatest needs are. You've mentioned, also, what you feel you need to accomplish in order to achieve the highest profit and at the same time serve your customers to their greatest satisfaction.

"You have been using our product for some time. Tell me what you like best and how we can improve our service to you."

It is essential that you probe for concerns. Often, what you don't like to hear is exactly what you should listen to most.

Use open-ended questions—and listen. If you spend all of your time talking, you'll uncover no new information. If you never walk except where there are tracks, you'll never make new discoveries.

I remember several years ago, one of my students in a workshop told me about a problem she was having. It was with the vice president of a company she had called on before and sold him a great deal of new machinery for their steel castings. That's why she couldn't understand why she was having so much trouble in getting a new visit.

She called. And she called. She sensed she was being rebuffed.

Finally, she did get through and the time was set for a visit. My student had scripted it well, rehearsed it carefully, and wrote out some of the questions she should ask. This was a big and important account.

But nothing goes according to script. That's one thing you can definitely count on.

My student began by doing all the right things. Probing, building rapport, asking about some personal issues they talked about in the last visit. (If you don't make careful notes about each visit, it puts you on the losing side.)

The conversation got to the point where it was time to talk about the product and reordering. Show time!

Here's what the buyer said. It isn't good.

"I've been wondering why you never came by after you made the sale. I kept thinking you would want to know how your machines are performing. I've been waiting for your call. I haven't heard from you once since I gave you that last order."

(You just know things are going to get worse. They did.)

"To begin with, the billing was all wrong. We had to call your finance office twice before we got the account straightened out.

"Then we discovered the damn thing didn't work like you said it would. I had to call in an engineer to correct it.

"A couple months ago, I receive a dumb letter from some vice president in your company. It's clear it's a form letter. It was sure written as if they didn't know I was a customer—and a big one. And all that time, I never heard from you."

My student was thinking of the Cheyenne warrior battle cry: It's a good day to die.

She had to respond immediately, not really certain what to say. She took her cue from the hero of the Indiana Jones films. When he was asked what he would do, his answer was: "I don't know. I'm making this up as I go."

"Ben, I am embarrassed. More than you can imagine. I thought I knew you so well, I'd let the office and our staff do some of the follow-up. I thought if you had any concerns or problems, you would let me know. I was obviously wrong. Terribly wrong.

"I've made a horrible blunder. Tell me more about what happened so we can get to the bottom of this." It's amazing what you don't learn when you don't listen.

Ben went on, nonstop, for the next 15 or 20 minutes. He finally wound down. And then something very special happened. When he got it all out of his system, he seemed to feel much better.

"Well, maybe it wasn't as bad as I've made out. And your machines are certainly better than your competitor's. Why did you decide to come by now? What did you want to talk with me about?"

They went on to have a warm and helpful discussion. Ben went on to place another order.

She made the sale. I am reminded that it is a spiritual axiom that God never closes one door without opening another. But sometimes the hallway in between is murder.

The secret was the student's thoughtful way of handling the complaint. It was her ability to listen with interest and concern. It often shows a fine command of the language to say nothing. She tuned the world out and tuned Ben in.

The student told me that she was swimming against a tough current. *"Finally, I broke through and I made the sale. I felt like I wanted to ask the choir to sing the doxology."*

There are several important lessons in all this. To begin with, you should document for your records every call and contact you make. If your company doesn't insist on this, do it for yourself. I tell my students if you don't record it, I don't consider it an activity or a call.

Bonnie McElveen Hunter says that objections and complaints are really your best friends. "If you don't work at eliciting objections from your buyers, you'll never know how they feel. That's why you have to probe and ask questions."

Open the door. Encourage any concerns or criticisms. If they don't surface, you will never know. Result: No sale.

If there is a problem (and this can happen), let your probable buyer air all her concerns. Encourage it. How else will you know if something is blocking the sale?

Wait your time. You will gain higher ground if you seek common ground. Listen attentively. When you feel the problem is completely aired, or nearly so—respond.

Work hard at putting people completely at ease. Make them feel important. Get them talking about themselves and their concerns. Probe.

Maintain eye contact and listen to how they feel. Understand fully that people are more likely to listen to you later if you listen to them first.

We know that intensive listening is the most important criterion in selling. More important than your dazzling presentation. More important than your relationship with the buyer (and that's plenty important). Even more important than the quality of your product.

Listen with your entire being. Listen with your eyes as well as your ears. Listen the sale.

14

It's Astounding What You Don't Sell When You Don't Ask

I KNOW WHAT IT'S LIKE. I can give personal testimony.

When I first started calling on folks, I was terrified. That's the truth of it. I could easily get through the early stages of the presentation. In fact, I was quite good.

I spoke with ease about my product and how it would serve the needs of the probable buyer. I had undisciplined enthusiasm for the fray and the venture.

But when it came to that frightening moment when I was to ask for the order, I froze. I felt like I had a chicken bone caught in my throat. All of a sudden I understood the song, "Bewitched, Bothered, and Bewildered."

Your initial sales calls will surely be a lot easier than Cal Turner's. His first experience was as a teenager in the family's store in Scottsville, Kentucky. He tells me that as a beginner, he got all the customers nobody else wanted.

"I remember trying to make a sale to this old, weathered farmer. He is struggling over buying a 39-cent pair of panties for his wife.

"I ask him what size she wears. He doesn't know. I tell him that if he doesn't know the size, we won't be able to find a pair of panties for him.

"'How big is she?' I ask.

"He points to my Aunt Ethel who also worked in the store. 'She's about her size.'

"Now I think I am getting somewhere.

"Aunt Ethel is our best clerk in the store. At the moment, she is waiting on an important customer. She is carrying a big armful of merchandise that she is about to ring up.

"'Ethel!' I yell. Have you ever been in a crowded room that suddenly becomes quiet? A Benedictine silence. My booming voice explodes across the crowded store.

"'Aunt Ethel, what size panties do you wear?'

"You can just imagine what happens next. She makes a noise that sounds like a wounded turkey. She drops all the merchandise on the floor that she is carrying. She races, red-faced, into the stockroom.

"Well . . . that doesn't work so I just hold up a pair of panties and the farmer tries to imagine whether they will fit or not."

I've had successful Fortune 500 executives who are in sales tell me about the problems they have had. They were able to make a dazzling presentation right up to finally asking for the order. Then they suffered the butterflies of the gladiator squinting at the emperor's box for a thumbs-up or a thumbs-down.

I've talked with prominent business leaders, college presidents, and multimillionaires who can achieve just about anything in life—except to ask for the order.

They have visions of Scylla—the sea nymph who is transformed into a six-headed monster.

I've even met some highly productive life insurance salespeople who at times feel the same agony. It's what John Steinbeck described as "the urge to be someplace else."

I've heard all of the reasons. And I've felt some of them myself.

"I'm afraid that the person I call on will say *no*."

"When I get ready to ask, I get all choked up."

Still another person told me he can't stand rejection.

But you'll never know unless you ask. The single overriding reason people give for why they haven't made the purchase is (you guessed it)—they weren't asked.

A monk asks a superior if it is permissible to smoke while praying. The superior responds with a quick rebuke: "Absolutely not."

The next day the monk asks the superior if it is acceptable to pray while smoking. "That is not only permissible, my son," says the superior, "it is admirable."

See, you never know unless you ask.

Step back and consider what happens if you do get *no* for an answer. I've learned it's not the solicitor who's being turned down.

In almost all cases, it means there isn't a meshing of the buyer's passions and interests with the value and use of the product. Go on to the next likely buyer. U.S. steep skiing pioneer and champion Chris Landry says: "If you fall and don't get up and go on, you die."

Often, there's nothing you can do about not making a sale. People buy for their reasons, not yours. It's their loss. Go on to the next likely buyer.

I tell my students that they're not smart enough to talk a reluctant buyer into a sale. And they shouldn't even try. That's not integrity selling.

Keep in mind there's a vast difference between principle-based selling and dazzle. Cultivate and court the former. Eschew the latter.

If you don't make the sale, go on to the next likely buyer. There's a whole world waiting to buy from you.

Melanie Sabelhaus tells me she found out early she was meant to be a salesperson. She went to work at Sears Roebuck right out of college.

"They put me in the wig department. I loved it. I found out I was really good at selling.

"A woman would come by looking at the wigs. She would end up leaving with three—blonde, redhead, and brunette. It was just plain fun."

Melanie ended up being the number one wig salesperson in the entire Sears chain. When the district manager asked her how she did it, she told him it was easy. "I just ask those wonderful women to buy my wigs."

What's clear to me is that there's no permanent damage to the salesperson who is turned down. You can survive. The important thing is that you ask.

Even if you don't make the sale, your spouse and friends love you. The dog greets you at the door, wildly wags his tail, and wets all over your shoes with joy. Life is good.

And one thing more of importance. If you're not getting rejections, it probably means you're not getting many acceptances either. You can't be in the wonderful game of selling without expecting some disappointments.

You're not finished when you don't make the sale. You're finished if you stop trying.

Aim for the moon. Even if you miss, you might grab a star along the way.

Every morning get up and look through the *Forbes* list of the richest people in America. If your name isn't on the list, get busy and go to work.

Here's a promise I make you. Your persistence will be rewarded. Your commitment and perseverance will achieve towering results.

Tenacity is a commitment to the end result regardless of what you have to endure. The race is not always to the swift—but to those who keep running—even through the pain and setbacks along the way.

You have to work at it. In selling, when dedication and asking become one, you reach the deep well where passion lives. You find fulfillment. And sales.

Wayne Gretzky, the great hockey all-time leading scorer, said: "One hundred percent of the shots I never take don't go in."

15

If You Don't Know Where You're Going, You'll Probably End Up Somewhere Else

I'M REMINDED THAT SELLING is a contact sport. You are judged on your wins.

Never lose track of the importance of good results. I remember hearing the president of a university at a victory celebration, speaking in glowing terms about the coach's highly successful football season. He gave great acclaim to the team and praised the coach profusely.

After the meeting, the beaming coach asked the president, "Would you still like me as much if we didn't win?"

I'd like you every bit as much, the president replied. "I'd just miss having you around."

You've come to that point in the visit when you must present the allure and appeal of your product. It's winning the sale. Winning with integrity.

You describe dramatically the value of your product to the buyer. It is complete with what Sam Goldwyn called, "warmth and charmth."

And this is important. You create a sense of urgency. (You don't want to have the decision delayed or put aside.)

You may wish to say something such as, "Here's why you might want to consider a decision now . . . ." Use your own language, whatever you're comfortable with. But move toward a decision.

Take no more than seven minutes to present the exciting opportunity your product presents. It is a dream of possibilities. Take fewer than seven minutes if possible.

Let me explain the seven minutes.

Oh, sure, you can take more time if you must. But not much. And at your own risk! All the research indicates this is about the maximum time a buyer can handle without tuning you out.

Ask anyone who produces videos professionally. They get paid for each minute of the video. The longer the video, the more they get paid. They still recommend a maximum of seven minutes. They will tell you that it mustn't be any longer than seven minutes. Some say five. Some say even fewer.

There's good reason for that. A longer video won't hold a person's attention for any longer.

This may seem surprising. After all, a video has a great deal going for it. A video has a musical background, professional narration, even sound effects. There's frenetic activity taking place. Heck, it looks like a Gypsy wedding going on in the background.

And with all this, professional videographers tell us the film still should be limited to six or seven minutes. So, if your dazzling presentation can be as inspiring as a professional video, you may take that much time. But be forewarned.

All right, so you're ready for your presentation. Proceed with the quiet efficiency of a night nurse.

This is the call to action. It's what I describe as, "working near the heart of things." Here are a few tips that will be helpful.

1. When you present the opportunity to the probable buyer, talk about the great benefits of your product—its value to the buyer—but sell with integrity.

Make certain when you talk about value, it's more than just about money. The cost is actually not the major buying motivator. Not if you make clear how your product will be of great advantage to the buyer. How it will bring untold pleasure and enhance life. Remember, sell the dream.

I like to tell the buyer of the satisfaction she will feel in using the product. Talk about results. That's what you're really selling—benefits and results.

2. Don't let features dominate the presentation. "We are number one in the marketplace" (who cares). "We have six widgets no other competitor has" (they'll never remember). "Ours uses less electricity than our competitors'" (not an exciting incentive to buying).

You get the idea. Sell the benefits and results. Not the features.

George Fisher was president of Kodak when it was at the very height of its revenue and profits. It dominated the film market. (How times have changed!)

I ask George one day what is the most important factor in Kodak's command of the marketplace. I am totally surprised by his response.

"We actually don't sell the quality of the film or the wide range of speeds that are available—more than any other film producer. Or the brilliancy of our luminescence. None of that. What we sell are memories. That's what film is all about."

3. Be careful not to let the dollars or cost reign over the presentation. Make it secondary to determining what most effectively fills the needs of the likely buyer.

Think about this for a moment. It's not really about money. Your job is to give reality to the dreams of the buyer. If it gets down to a contest about cost and bargaining—you've lost.

You're not trying to manipulate the buyer. Tricky negotiations, fast-talking, and smart gimmicks are all repugnant.

That's not integrity selling. You may be able to unload your product. But you will never be a truly successful salesperson.

Instead, understand full well that you're helping the buyer make an investment that will bring pleasure and satisfaction. When you sell with integrity, the buyers have complete confidence they made the right decision.

Cal Turner Jr. tells me that he wants the customer to have a joyful experience. "That's really what drives us. Not to make a sale but to have a completely happy customer."

It's important to keep in mind that people don't like to be sold. But they do like to buy.

Don't sell the product. Talk about the return on their investment.

4. The case for your product must have relevancy, drama, and emotional appeal. You may well ask what emotional appeal would there be if you are selling, let's say, new accounting software. Well, if you're selling to someone who is drowning in accounting headaches or other IT problems and not meeting deadlines—the new software could have great emotional appeal.

Successful selling is not the cold calls you make or meeting a quota. It is the lighting of a fire.

5. Most of all, there must be some sense of urgency. You don't want the decision to buy to be postponed.

The stakes are high, time is pressing, and the buyer's needs are great. Your product is the effective answer. It is the solution. Now is the time for the buyer to respond.

6. Shy away from talking about big, abstract numbers. They will not help you make the sale. Actually, they're a distraction.

"Last year, we had over 500,000 policyholders." Take that, for example. Who cares about the number of policyholders? Your buyer wants to know how the insurance impacts him.

I like to think of what I call the "Anne Frank concept." It's hard to get your arms around and identify with the three million Jewish children who died in the Holocaust. But it's easy to be completely engulfed with the Anne Frank story. When making a presentation, think Anne Frank.

Above all else, integrity leads the list. I've saved the most important until last. It is the incontestable ingredient.

David McCullough is a Pulitzer Prize winner and many times a *New York Times* best-selling author. He was asked what attributes characterize a successful person in any field. He lists seven.

But read what he says is most important. "In the last analysis, character counts above all. It provides the foundation for everything else."

Character counts. Sell with integrity.

Success is a moving target. Bring your passion, commitment, and joy to your calls. People take heart when you give them yours.

A supremely successful salesperson realizes the essential elements of integrity and self-motivation. Integrity is the key to the ignition switch that drives the sale.

16

There Are No Shortcuts to Anyplace Worth Going

I'M GOING TO GIVE YOU a system that ensures your success. It really works. Mark this page. When you finish the book, you'll want to come back to this chapter.

This is going to take a little extra time on your part. Keep in mind that winners are those who make a practice of doing the things losers won't take time to do. You are going to be a winner.

Here's what I do before every sales call I make. Every visit. I suggest you do it, also. I want you to embrace this design like your chalice, and consider these steps as some sort of a sacred sacrament.

I make a lot of contacts and calls. I follow the same pattern I'm about to describe on every visit. I've discovered that if I do this faithfully, I'm properly prepared. Even if the visit doesn't go according to plan (and they often don't), I know I'll not miss an opportunity.

Typically, I do all of this on a 4 × 6 card. That just seems to work for me. When I mentioned this at a recent seminar, one of my students told me I was 20 years behind the times.

"Haven't you heard about computers?" she chided. I told her I was making progress. In the past, I had been using 3 × 5 cards.

But of course, choose whatever works for you. Use your BlackBerry, iPhone, iPad, or whatever. I like 4 × 6 cards because I can pull them quickly in and out of my pocket.

I carry the cards with me. I always take one last-minute look before I ring the doorbell or am at the desk of the receptionist. Everything possible I'm about to use on my visit goes on my index card.

1. **I list everything I know about my likely buyer**. This includes, of course, all prior purchases of the product from my company. I also want to know something about his family, think about some of my other customers who may know the family, information about his competitors, disposable income (if I can get some sort of an idea about that), and that sort of information.

2. **I indicate the objective I hope to achieve** during the visit. Knowing my objective is essential. Here's an example.

   I am going to ask Peter about switching his corporate account to our bank. I'll talk with him about the very special service we provide corporate clients, the senior staff who will be assigned to work with him, and the savings we can offer in actual out-of-pocket costs.

   Here's what I need to do on this visit. I won't leave without probing how Peter feels about the value of our service and the line of credit we can extend. This visit is to get me one step closer to making the sale. I understand that it may take another call to finally get the order. Or perhaps several.

   The step I just described is critical. If you don't have a specific objective, you won't know where you're going. You'll be like the fellow on the Los Angeles freeway who says to his wife: "Don't worry, honey, that we're lost. We're making good time."

3. **I give some thought as to what I'm going to talk about**. I avoid what the Russian poet Andre Voznesensky calls the dribble of blah-blah-blah. In integrity selling, you write your own script. Just make certain you know how you want the plot to turn out.

   No razzle-dazzle. Be on point. Albert Einstein once wrote: "You do not really understand something unless you can explain it to your grandmother."

4. **I think about how I will express the cost of the product**. I actually say it out loud several times before I make a visit. Go ahead, say it!

5. **I list the questions I feel I should ask** in order to get the kind of information I need. *How do you feel about our product? How do you feel it will make your life easier? Which brand are you using now? What do you like best about what we've discussed?* (Note: All of these questions are open-ended. You can't answer any of them with a simple *yes* or *no*.)

6. **I make a list of the kind of concerns and objections that are most likely to be raised** by the probable buyer. I am as specific as possible. I write down the answers.

   Let me tell you about my strong personal preference. I do not take notes during a visit. Not unless there is some detail I simply must record. I don't take notes because I am engaging the buyer in a pleasant conversation. After the visit, I make notes like crazy. I put them on my index card for future reference.

7. **I determine what, if anything, I am going to leave behind in the way of material or a written proposal.** Keep in mind it might be more productive to leave nothing. It's effective and important to follow the visit the next day with a special letter and material.

   Don't put it off. Follow up immediately with a letter or phone call. Social scientists tell us that within 48 hours, people remember only 42 percent of what you've said. In 30 days, they forget 91 percent of your dazzling presentation.

8. **I think carefully and list the reasons why the person I'm calling on should buy**. Make certain that it's a win-win-win for the buyer, your company, and you. If it isn't, it's not selling with integrity.

I want you to understand that your desire to make the sale is totally compatible with ethics and integrity. You don't make promises you can't keep. Never! All great salespeople achieve successful results without overclaiming or stretching the truth.

9. **I speak about the outcomes and results that will accrue to the buyer.** Dortch Oldham puts it in focus.

    "With the people we're calling on, I want them to know that they're not just buying a set of books or something for the home. I want them to know how this purchase enhances their life. Perhaps changes their life. For the whole family."

10. **I think about any closing strategies that might be particularly helpful.** ("I'm going to send over some material that you'll enjoy reading before I visit again." Or: "Is there anything at all I haven't thought to ask that may be important in your making a decision? Have I left out anything at all?")

You may well ask if recording all this in your BlackBerry or iPad (me on my 4 × 6 card) is worth doing. "Do I really need to do it on every single visit?"

The answer is an emphatic *yes*. There are no shortcuts to anyplace worth going. If you don't know the direction you need to take, there isn't a road that will take your there.

I've been doing the 4 × 6 cards so long that I'd feel lost if I didn't. (It's like flossing your teeth. It's a pain, but you know it's good for you and the right thing to do.) It takes a little extra time and effort, but when I finish my 4 × 6 card, I'm really ready. You will be, too.

If you're not properly prepared, you greatly diminish the probability of the sale. You will have a buyer who thinks they can only find fault with three things in that presentation of yours—the beginning, the middle, and the end.

But that's not you. You're ready.

You've done your homework and recorded everything you need for your visit. Everything is wrapped in a perfect package for your sales call, with few strings remaining untied. You're ready to ring the bell or announce yourself to the receptionist.

There is nothing that can take the place of the delight and wonder of making the sale. You are perfectly prepared. You're going to make the sale. You are home. You know this zip.

You are going to hear three of the most beautiful words in the English language—"I'll buy it."

17 | Know Your Product, but It's Testimony that Persuades

THE TIME HAS COME. You are prepared. You're making the call. You are facing the buyer.

You're ready to begin. You remember Lewis Carroll's Alice: "I don't see how he can ever finish if he doesn't begin."

You are psyched. You've set the stage and done a superb job of getting ready. As perfectly correct as the blind embossing on the letterhead of a prestigious Boston law firm.

You begin with a positive attitude. You are with the probable buyer. You probe and ask open-ended questions. And you listen.

The successful salesperson listens. You listen assertively to your buyer's ideas, needs, aspirations, and wishes. These are the forces that motivate a sale. You need to explore.

Now comes one of the most telling and effective parts of your presentation. I want you to give testimony to your own use and feeling about the product.

Obviously, you may not be able to testify to your own beneficial use if you are selling, for instance, the e-Studio 1351 Hewlett-Packard duplicator (the monster cranks out 285 pages a minute). Or, let's say, the Rolls Royce turbine engine for the latest Boeing aircraft. This presents, however, an excellent opportunity to use a reference—one of your satisfied customers.

Here's an example of what you might say:

"I asked Fred Johnson if I might use his name. He heads the Engineering Department at Erie's General Electric plant. He said he wanted me to tell everyone I possibly can that our equipment is the best he has ever seen or used. And he's used plenty. He says to tell everyone that the cost is right, there's no maintenance, and the service is superb."

Then, if it's appropriate give your probable buyer Fred's phone number. And provide another testimony or two.

But if it's a consumer product you're selling, you know how powerful it can be to have the salesperson give personal testimony. I was in a store recently and tried on three pairs of running shoes. I was staring at the three pairs, undecided.

The salesperson who brought the shoes out to me comes back. He picks up a pair of shoes from the three I am looking at.

"This particular New Balance shoe came in first in *Runner's World* magazine. So I decided I would try a pair," he says.

"I've never worn a pair like this in all my running. They're light yet they have all the cushioning you could possibly want. I pronate, just like you told me you do—and they solved my problem. When I wear them, I feel like I'm floating."

Guess which pair I bought!

The shoe salesman reminded me of something important. Note it well. The job of a salesman is not to make a sale. It is to make a customer.

So if you sell a consumer product like, for instance, garden equipment for the home, vacuum cleaners at Wal-Mart, life insurance, vitamins at the local health store, or whatever—give positive testimony to your own use.

To every ounce of your presentation, give a pound of personal testimony.

This seems obvious but it's worth repeating because it's so important. Why should anyone buy your product if you don't care enough to buy it yourself.

Stanley Marcus once gave me a list of the products he thought were the best in their specific category. Premier.

He mentioned Cohiba cigars, a Mont Blanc pen (No. 149), a watch from IWC, and Oxxford suits. There were more items but I don't remember the others.

A month or so later, I'm sitting next to a guy on a plane who is belted in and still wearing his jacket. I notice because most men take off their jackets before the flight begins.

But what I really notice is that this is a beautiful jacket. A beautiful soft cloth, good color, perfect tailoring.

"That's a great looking jacket," I tell him.

He opens the jacket so I can see the label. "It's an Oxxford," he tells me. "That's all I buy now. They are the most comfortable and best fitting I've ever worn. And they never seem to wrinkle."

Guess what my next suit was!

It's the power of personal testimony. Use it in every presentation. It's what Charles Swindoll writes about in his *Simple Faith*—"lighting your fire and shaking your salt."

Giving testimony is important because it provides credence to your own enthusiasm and delight in the product. It gives witness and proof. There's no mistaking it. It's as obvious as the feathers on your chin that mean you ate the parakeet!

Attesting to your own personal use does something else, too. It takes all you've said in the entire meeting about the product and its extraordinary value and narrows the focus to something quite personal.

You have positioned it in terms of its impact on you. You are strumming mystical chords. Theodore Roosevelt called it: "Giving unambiguous demonstration of where I firmly stand."

18

If You Think You'll Lose, You're Lost

NOW YOU'VE COME to the moment of truth—when you must ask for the order. So far you've done an outstanding job.

You probed. You asked questions. You listened. You presented a dramatic and urgent opportunity. And you gave testimony to your own use of the product or provided witness to someone else's.

Everything you've done has led to this moment. There's suspense. Plenty. Butterflies? You bet. But that's okay. We all feel it. I still do when I'm ready to ask for the order.

The stress in the room crackles. It's raining stress and strain. The heartbeat quickens.

And your buyer actually feels the same pangs of angst, too. There's plenty of tension between the two of you. The buyer feels it because she's not certain what's coming next and for how much. And she wonders how she will respond. Even if it's not a personal purchase, the corporate buyer also feels the uneasiness.

You feel like one of the brothers in *Beau Geste*, the classic film about the French Foreign Legion. He touches his brother to see if they're still alive.

And finally you're ready to transform your entire visit into the invitation to buy. The words I use are fairly simple:

"I would like you to consider purchasing our . . ."

That's how easy it is. Not much magic to all of that. Simply: "I would like you to consider purchasing our . . ."

Those are the words that work most effectively for me. But find whatever feels best and most comfortable for you. Sing the words to your own song. For instance, "I would like to invite you . . ."

I am sitting across the desk one day from W. Clement Stone. He's the genius who began selling insurance by walking into a Chicago skyscraper. He started at the top floor, working his way down from floor to floor, calling in every office on every floor. His practice was to just walk into an office without an appointment.

I'm sitting in his office. He's advancing in years but as vital as ever.

He inhales deeply on his Cuban cigar. I'm at the feet of the nation's greatest salesman and the father of the concept of Positive Mental Attitude. He wrote the book.

Positive Mental Attitude. He wrote about it. He talked about it. He lived it.

We talk about what makes a great salesman. He says it's hard work, persistence, and integrity. Buyers need to have confidence in the person who calls on them.

"You are one of the wealthiest men in the country," I say. "And regarded as one of the greatest salesman. Tell me how you got started. What's so special about the way you train all your salespeople?"

With that, Stone jumps out of his chair. He grabs my arm and leads me out of the office.

"Come with me. I'll show you how we do it." We're racing to a stairway.

We go down a couple flights of stairs. We come to a hallway. He points to an office and says this is where we should start.

We walk into the office. Clem tells the receptionist he wants to talk to the manager. "I'm Clement Stone. I'd like to speak to the person in charge of the office."

We're ushered in. (What magic did he use? I've never had that easy an entrance.)

Stone chats a bit to find out about the manager's needs and desires. There's not a lot of small talk. There's an economy of time spent on gaining rapport. (I actually would have taken more time.)

Now this is the best part. This is what I want you to note.

He is ready to ask for the order. (I could sense the manager knew it was coming.)

"Do I have permission to ask you to protect your family?" (*Do I have your permission*! Where the devil did that come from? Remember, I wrote earlier to use the words that work best for you.)

"Yes, of course, Mr. Stone," the manager says. The ask was made. There was a bit more talk. Not much. The manager said yes. He bought a policy.

The point is that the words he used worked remarkably well for Clement Stone. But it may seem horribly awkward for you. Recite your own hymn. Just be certain you ask.

Let's have a moment of truth. I've always been a bit suspicious of how easy it was for Stone to barge into an office and tell the receptionist he wanted to see the manager. I'm thinking I know he started his company this way, but was he setting me up? Did the people in that office know Stone? Did his reputation get him into the manager's office?

I finally decided it didn't matter. Just watching Clement Stone in action, exercising his positive mental attitude—well, at that young stage in my life of selling, that visit was worth a college graduate degree.

Do you notice something about Clement Stone and my visit? There was not a moment's hesitation. He was crackling with positive vibrations. All the supremely successful salespeople believe if you think you can't, you won't—if you think you can, you will. It was Henry Ford who first said that 70 years ago. It's just as true today.

(Oh, by the way—you may be wondering about the Cuban cigar I mentioned earlier. Stone found out, years before through his contacts, that there would likely be an embargo against Cuba. He bought four warehouses of his favorite Cuban Montecristo cigars. He had them shipped to Chicago to buildings he constructed with perfect climate control. He told me he bought a 20-year supply.)

Okay. Back to you.

You asked for the order. You wait. The moment is suddenly flooded with silence, a thundering quiet.

The next point is very important. *Do not fill in the silence.* You observe the silence of a Trappist monk.

Wait for the buyer to speak. It may seem like hours. There are times I felt the silence was so painfully long I could be excused to go for a walk. Or do hand puppets!

You want to break the silence. You want to say anything. I've found, however, that *nothing* is a good thing to say . . . and always a clever way of saying it.

We learn from the great author Guy de Maupassant. He wrote that success is simply thoughtful silence.

Resist the temptation—don't talk. If you do, you may never know how the buyer really feels about the product, the cost, or its value to her. The secret of success, I've learned, is holding on for a minute longer.

I have found it is never more than 10 or so seconds. Even though it seems longer. Your buyer will respond. That's when you know whether or not you made the sale.

Not every sale follows a proper structure. That's why I say it's more an art than a science. Take a lesson from the young salesman I'm going to tell you about.

He had only been in the field a week or so when he managed to get an appointment with one of the most important and busiest executives in Minneapolis—Bob Kenney, CEO of General Mills.

Bob told me this story. I heard him tell others of the same experience. He was certain he was set-up, but he thought it was funny. And a good learning experience. It was Bob's nature to laugh at himself.

"I'm the brand new membership director at the Minneapolis Club," the young man told Bob in introducing himself. He went on. "I'm a complete novice at this. I'm supposed to ask you if you would be interested in joining the club. I was pretty certain you wouldn't be. And I don't know how to sell anything.

"I've only been on the job a couple weeks and I must tell you that I'm darn nervous. I just feel I'm not going to make a sale and I'm not even certain why you gave me the time."

"Well, young man," Kenney said, "you're never going to make a sale with that kind of an attitude. You have got to be positive. Every time you make a call, you have got to feel that you are going to make a sale.

"You need to tell me what an outstanding value the club is. Tell me most Minneapolis' leaders are members. Talk about the special programs you offer and that the club has the best kitchen in town.

"Be positive. Do you understand, young man? You need to feel you can call on anyone and make the sale. I hope I've helped you."

"You have indeed," said the young salesman. "Now I have much more confidence. Will you join the club, sir?" Kenney did!

I'm reminded of the secret of a supremely successful salesperson: Triumph is just "umph" added to "try."

19

Climb the Ladder of Success One Objection at a Time

YOU'VE GONE THROUGH YOUR PRESENTATION. You established an effective bond by probing and asking questions. You gained rapport.

You encouraged your likely buyer to do most of the talking. I've told you that you will have your greatest success if you talk only 25 percent of the time. That's the hard part for most salespeople. We love to talk.

But your job is to get the buyer to talk. That's how you pick up selling clues and buying incentives.

Note this well. The need to be heard, which some take for granted, turns out to be the single most powerful motivating force in human nature. People want to be heard. Your buyer wants you to listen.

Studies are quite clear. People buy from a salesperson who listens.

You listen. You are making the presentation. You felt during the entire time there was a great endorsement of your product.

You are encouraged because the buyer seems intent and raises appropriate questions. You notice that he nods approvingly and smiles throughout your presentation.

Everything is properly in place.

You come to those simple words that transform your entire visit into an invitation to buy. You review once more (very briefly) the important benefits to your buyer. Then, those words that effectively convert your meeting into an ask: *"I would like you to consider. . ."*

I often don't repeat the cost. But not always. Remember, it's not about the product. Or the cost. It's about the buyer. You ask. Then you pause.

The response is not entirely surprising.

"I'm not really certain, Jerry. It's something I'll need to think over."

Good!

What? you ask. Good?

Yes, good!

You couldn't have hoped for a better response—unless it was something like: "As a matter of fact Jerry, I'm going to buy five of your gizmos." (Oh sure! I've been waiting for that to happen.)

You now have an opportunity to learn how the buyer really feels about your product and your request. You also need to find out if there are any problems or concerns.

You must now find out what your buyer is thinking. You are ready to ask my Three Magic Questions. That's all there are, just three.

My typical reply to the buyer's "I need to think it over" is something like this:

"Of course, Mary, you're going to need more time to think this over. I've suggested a purchase you might not have been thinking about. But let me just ask you . . ."

I will then proceed to ask Mary my Three Magic Questions to determine the reason for any hesitancy:

1. Is it the *product*?
2. Is it the *cost*?
3. Is it the *timing*?

Before I leave, I have to know how she feels about these three issues. When I find the answer to that, I'm on my way to making the sale. And so I probe.

"As we were talking, you seemed to indicate a great interest in this model of the Ford. It seemed to be a perfect car to meet your needs. Am I right about that?" (Is it the product?)

Mary says something like:

"Yes, I think it's a wonderful car."

Great! I'm on my way through the first question. Let's have a drum roll, please.

"By the way, I could have had my pick of any car to show you—and I chose the very car you're thinking of buying (subtle affirmation). It is the greatest car I've ever owned (personal testimony). I feel wrapped in luxury although it's not an expensive car. I already have 22,000 miles on it and haven't had a single problem.

"The more we talked, the more I was certain you really liked the car. I remember when you sat down behind the wheel, you felt like you were in the cockpit of a 747. And the four-speaker Bose sound system blew you away. You loved it.

"You felt good about the gas mileage, too—34 miles a gallon is the best of any car in this field. (Note: She made no comments to the salesperson about the mechanical features of the car—so there was no need for him to dwell on this.) *It seems to be the perfect car for you. Am I right about that?"*

I want to confirm that there's no problem with the product.

"Oh yes, I love the car." (I'm ready to sing hymns.)

Now I have to test the cost. This could be the breaking point.

"When you came in, you told me what you hoped to spend for a car."

She says: "I know we talked about the cost. But now I think this is a little more than I think I can handle. (Ouch! I may be in trouble. I need to find out if this is going to nix the sale.) Gee, I don't know if I should spend that much."

So the cost is a hurdle I have to overcome. But the prospects of a sale still seem good to me. The stars all seem to be singing together for joy. I think it's a *maybe* on its way to a *yes*. So here's my response:

"You know what. That car is perfect for you. I'm not going to let you buy a lesser model from me (affirming I'm not interested in just making a sale of some sort) *and be unhappy.*

"By the way, I could have taken the Bose out to save you money but I won't do that—you loved it so."

The cost may be a problem, but perhaps that can be solved by raising a question about the timing (the third Magic Question).

"Let me ask this, Mary. Instead of taking 36 months to pay this off, if you had an extra 12 months to make payments, would that make a difference?"

Mary extends the payments to 48 months. The sale is made.

You see what I did, and what you need to do. The initial response from Mary didn't lead us anywhere. It was certainly better than a flat-out *no*. But it didn't give any indication if there were issues still needing to be resolved.

The question you need to determine is whether her comments are a *maybe* on its way to a *no* or a *maybe* on its way to a *yes*. In Mary's case, it was a matter of the cost. She loved the product. The timing made it possible.

You need to know the answers to these Three Magic Questions. Even if I get a *no* early in the visit, I ask the same questions (the only dumb questions are the ones you don't ask).

I find very often that a *no* early in the conversation is really a *maybe*, on its way to a *yes*. It's up to you to find out. You ask the Three Magic Questions. You make the decision to succeed.

I once asked Stanley Marcus how he felt when someone said *no* to his request to buy a product. Stanley is, after all, considered one of the greatest salesmen of the past century. What is it like for Stanley to get a *no*?

He said: "I never take no for an answer. Even if the person dies, I consider it only a maybe!"

20

Objections Aren't Bitter if You Don't Swallow Them

CONFESSION IS GOOD for the soul.

I must admit when I first started in selling, I hated objections. I felt like the Tin Man cowering before the Wizard of Oz.

There I was, just finishing a flawless and dazzling presentation. And now I can just see my buyer winding up, ready to deliver a whammo objection.

I want to run for cover. What do you do when you stand at the crossroads and all of the signposts are gone?

But what I realize now is that objections are truly your best friends. They're often the way probable buyers mask their concerns about needing help or more information.

I now encourage objections. I do! Three cheers. I probe for hidden or unspoken ones. The sales call is round. What seems like the end may only be the beginning.

Here's what I know. You won't be able to sell your product until every concern is satisfied, no matter how inappropriate or trivial.

The objections may feel like a personal assault, perhaps even an attack. But they're not. Your first impulse is to be defensive, to strike back. But don't.

Remember, your job isn't to prevail, knock down, and win. That's not integrity selling. Your job is to resolve the objection.

I like the story of the foreman who was very hard-working and conscientious. But he hadn't received a promotion in 12 years. Asked if he had an explanation for his failure to advance, he replied: "Many years ago, I had an argument with my supervisor. I won."

Your success will depend on your ability to go from one objection to another without loss of your optimism or enthusiasm. An objection is the master key to opening the door to making the sale.

Probe some more, ask questions, dig deeper into the concern. Remain poised, interested, completely understanding, confident, and positive. Just do what it says on the back of the Hellman's mayonnaise jar: Keep cool and don't freeze!

Keep in mind that your job isn't to beat down the objection. It is to resolve it and win over the buyer. You can't leave your meeting until all objections are out on the table.

When I first started selling, objections were the worst part of the call. I felt the same pain that must have befallen Albert Payson Terhune. When he was savagely bitten by his pet collie. He was a breeder of collies and the author of numerous books on collies, including *Lassie*.

But what I finally learned is that objections are like a grindstone. They either grind you down or polish you up. What happens depends on you.

If you don't respond to all possible objections, you're not going to make the sale. Don't worry about objections. Embrace them. They are the most important tools in your sales kit.

Successful salespeople are like teabags. You never see their true strength until they're in hot water.

That's why I say—three *no's* and you're halfway to a *yes*. Remember, Columbus was turned down six times before he made the sale.

For every objection, there is an effective response. You just have to find it. When you come to a roadblock, take a detour. An objection is what you see when you take your eyes off the objective.

The most successful salesperson develops the ability to deal with massive doses of rejection. High achievers, supremely successful salespeople rarely think about objections or failure as being final or fatal. Instead, they believe in delayed success. A loser says, "I'll never sell it." A winner says, "I can't sell it yet."

21 | No Isn't an Answer, It's a Question

I CALL THIS NEXT STEP the "Pleasant and Persistent Pursuit of Getting the Order." You certainly should be persistent. And when you're selling with integrity, it must be enjoyable—for both you and the buyer.

Expect some objections. They will be your best friends in making the sale.

I'm going to give you some typical objections you may encounter and the sort of response I would give. Let's say you're selling a vacuum cleaner. For our purposes, that will serve as a good example.

I think of vacuum cleaners because since 1924, and to this very day, the Electrolux vacuum cleaner has been sold door-to-door. It is what makes it the largest-selling vacuum cleaner in the country.

Their salesmen have always been very effective. The objections they often receive are generic. They are pretty much what you might hear, no matter what the product. That's why I'm using the vacuum cleaner salesman to illustrate my point.

In this chapter, I'll also give you a formula I often use. It's quite simple: Feel, Felt, Found. I think you'll find it extremely helpful.

Feel indicates clearly that you really have listened to the person's objection. It also says you sympathize with the buyer. You can identify with the concern. You and the buyer are beginning to bond. *Felt* signals that you empathize with the buyer's situation. *Found* demonstrates that there is a happy solution.

It really works. Using this formula when you get an objection is like jumping off a cliff and building your wings on the way down. I'll give you examples in a moment.

One word of caution. I wouldn't use this approach more than twice in a session with a person, three times at the most. After awhile, your likely buyer will say: No more of that feel, felt, found business. I understand what you're doing!

Here are three examples:

(Your first thought when you hear an objection is *Ars Moriendi*—*The Art of Dying*. But you know better. You understand that objections are your best friends. If you don't hear any concerns, you'll never know how the likely buyer really feels. So you respond.)

Objection: "I can't make a decision now. I'll have to talk it over with my husband."

Response: "I'm not surprised at all. I suspect you weren't giving a lot of thought to buying a vacuum before I called on you.

"Take your time to think it over and talk with your husband. Let's set a time now that I might be able to see you and your husband together. I want to be able to show him how much cleaner you can get the house and how you can destroy some of the germs that hide in the carpet. I'd like to tell him, also, how much easier it will make your life."

- Or use: Feel, Felt, Found.

Response: "I know how you *feel* about making a decision on the spot. As a matter of fact, I hate to be pinned down like that myself. Before I joined Electrolux, my wife was asked to buy a vacuum and I wasn't home. She *felt* exactly like you.

"It was really her decision but she wanted an opportunity to review the purchase in more detail with me and perhaps check on what some other vacuum cleaners feature. She just needed a little more breathing space.

"I *found* that a small delay was helpful and it meant she and I didn't get carried away with the excitement of hearing the salesman's presentation and the demonstration of the cleaner.

"Actually, it was pretty astonishing. The salesman vacuumed our living room rug with our old vacuum. He emptied the bag. I thought the rug was clean. Then he vacuumed with the Electrolux. When he emptied the bag, there was three times the dirt we usually get.

"That's when I decided right there and then to be an Electrolux salesman. I can tell you, it's the very best vacuum on the market. I found that out by buying one myself before I joined the firm," (personal testimony).

Objection: "Leave the material with me. I'll look it over and then mail in my order."

Response: "There's no question in my mind you would mail the order in. And I'm so pleased you're showing an interest in buying the vacuum. But having you as a valued customer is so important to me—and I hope to you—that I want to be present to discuss the next step with you. I am committed to doing everything I can to personally follow through with my customers and give them the proper service—before and after the sale.

"That's why I want to be certain to talk with you once more about the order. I want to go over again some of the unique features so you'll be able to put them to immediate use.

"When is a good time to see you again? Pull out your calendar. Can we get back together in another week?" (By the way, never leave a visit without a commitment to something—a sale or a new date for a meeting.)

- Or: Use Feel, Felt, Found.

Response: "I know how you *feel*. When the salesman called on me, I *felt* I might be pressed into signing something I wouldn't be happy with afterward. That's why I suggested that you take another week to think it over.

"I told you about the person who called on my wife and me to buy a vacuum. He explained how important it was to think about any questions we might still have. And he wanted to demonstrate some of the features again.

"Don't worry, I'm not going to try to talk you into signing an order. I'm not smart enough to do that. And I wouldn't want to. I *found* that the second visit was actually very helpful. In my own case, I still had a few questions I needed some answers for, and I got them in that session.

"And as it turned out, we made some special arrangements for the way this would be paid for that worked to my advantage. I really wouldn't have known about all of this if we hadn't had that second visit. Take out your calendar and let's look at a date when we can get together again. How about next week?"

Objection: "This is a terrible time for me to spend money on something like this. I've got a daughter's wedding and a kid going through college."

Response: "I know what you're going through. I've been there myself. You can get pretty stretched out, can't you?

"I think the important thing for us to discuss is how interested you are about the vacuum cleaner and what you'd be inclined to do if you didn't have these extra expenses right now.

"If you feel as good about the vacuum as I believe you do, it'll be easy to work out the timing so that you don't have to make the first payment for 60 days—then we can even stretch out the rest of the payments.

"The important thing for you to think about is how you feel about the vacuum. Let's talk for a moment about what you would like to do if you didn't have those expenses now."

- Or: Use Feel, Felt, Found.

Response: "I know how you *feel*. I really do. You think that some of those costs and the tuition will never end. Thankfully, they do. There are a lot of folks I've called on who *felt* the same way you do and so here's what we've arranged.

"I *found* that what is most important is for you to agree that this little beauty is going to make your life so much easier. The vacuum is so light you can carry it up and down the stairs with ease. It gets into places no other vacuum can. And it folds beautifully in the closet—it takes almost no space.

"I'll come by again and we can talk about how you want to handle the payments and I can answer any questions you might have.

"We *found* that what's most important is to determine what you would like to do when you have fewer of these unusual expenses. Just let me know what you would intend to do if it weren't for the expenses. Maybe we can work something out. I know you want the vacuum.

"How would you feel if we could stretch the payments out an extra several months? How does that work for you?"

You'll be surprised at what I tell you next. It's an important verity, so note it well. Zig Ziglar, the high potentate of selling and the most prolific author on salesmanship, gives us the following information:

- Forty-three percent of salespeople give up after the first objection, take their leave, and go on their merry (and unproductive) way.

- Seventeen percent give up after the second objection. They just can't handle rejection.
- Four percent hold out until the third objection. Then they can't take it any longer, throw in the towel, and leave.

But here's what you need to know: Ziglar tells us that 74 percent of the buyers voice three objections before making their decision to buy. That means 64 percent of those I just described weren't even in the ballgame. Shame on them. They didn't make the sale.

That's why I say that three no's means you're halfway to a yes.

Objections are tough. But it's essential you probe to find out if there are any problems or issues you must overcome.

Dortch Oldham said to me that persistence is the key. You mustn't give up too soon. Some buyers actually want to give the appearance that they don't want to give in too easily. The objections can be addressed and then thoughtfully dismissed. That's integrity selling.

Let me tell you about a mistake I made for years. I would finish my presentation—perhaps short of an Oscar, but not bad at all. My probable buyer was smiling, his head nodding in agreement the entire time.

I followed all the steps I described in my earlier chapters—every step but one. I didn't probe. I didn't ask my Three Magic Questions.

In Schubert's *Der Hirt Auf Dem Felsen*, he writes: "I am consumed with grief. My joy is at an end. Hope has deserted me." I know the feeling!

But believe me, objections are your friends because they lead you to the sale. But there are times, no matter what you do, you are simply not going to be able to overcome all objections. Don't despair. Go on to the next likely buyer.

I believe in catching stars. I'm willing, and I want you to be also. I want you to take the risk of falling down, getting up, and trying again.

22 | The Horrifying 10

IF YOU DON'T MAKE THE SALE—and
won't—there is often 1 of 10 reasons you we
There may be more than the 10 when you do
these are the primary ones.

You may find it takes a sales call or two before you're able to
avoid them all. I know in my own solicitations, when I failed,
my immediate instinct was to pull the shades and devote the rest
of my life to reading the collected works of Emily Dickinson.

But I soon learned that the mark of a motivated and
supremely successful salesperson is the ability to distinguish
a temporary setback from a defeat. I've been blessed with an
invincible spirit. You will be, too, if you stick with it.

It's not a matter of whether you get knocked down. You
will. It's whether you get up again. And I do.

I've made sales calls where I've had them dancing in the
aisles. Yes, dancing in the aisles—running for the exit. I struck
out. But I just kept making my calls.

One of my students at a seminar told me he couldn't figure it
out—why he lost the sale. "I had them laughing their asses off."
I told him that was the problem. "You weren't selling asses."

Giving up is the ultimate tragedy. Failure is not the
crime—low aspirations are.

Here are the 10 tragic reasons to avoid.

1. You Didn't Make the Call to Set Up the Visit

You committed the most grievous act of all. You never tele-
phoned to set up the visit. You kept putting it off.

You stared at the phone. And you stared. And you stared.
You hoped it would ring so you wouldn't have to punch in the

...mber. But it didn't ring. You gathered up your material and walked away. Coward!

To paraphrase some words from the *Book of Common Prayer*—distressed by what we have done, horrified by what we have left undone, and convinced there is no hope for us.

Here's another trap. Let's say you do the kind of selling that doesn't require a phone call to set up the visit.

You keep postponing making your contacts. You wake up later than you should and you find a dozen things you simply must do before leaving the house. You check your e-mails, Google for a recipe, rearrange the piles on your desk. Good grief! You even floss your teeth.

You may be brilliant, but you are also erratic and undependable. You're not steady, not committed to the work. You are a person who jaywalks through life.

You probably should consider a different profession. You may not have the initiative and dedication to be a successful salesperson.

Or let's say you're a clerk in the department at Neiman-Marcus that sells wedding dresses. Stanley Marcus shared this lesson with me.

"The other day," he tells me, "a lovely young woman and her mother came into our downtown store to look at wedding dresses. They are very interested in one gown in particular. The young lady looks stunning in it.

"But they didn't buy it. They discussed it back and forth but couldn't make a decision. 'I'd like a day to think it over,' the bride-to-be said, 'and maybe look at Saks and Nordstrom.'"

(Shame on the clerk. She didn't ask the Three Magic Questions.)

"If you don't ask any questions," Stanley continues, "you're in trouble. The clerk should have asked questions before she ever started showing any wedding gowns. Questions about the bride, the groom, how big a wedding, what the wedding party will be wearing, and that sort of thing (mistake No. 1). She didn't ask for the young woman or her mother's phone number (mistake No. 2). And she didn't call (mistake No. 3) to follow up. If she had, the clerk could have said, "I'm still holding that dress for Deborah. She'll be beautiful in it . . . ."

2. Inadequate Preparation

You didn't take time to prepare or to know your buyer. And you didn't practice. You thought you could wing it.

I know what that's like. When I first started out, I didn't prepare. I thought somehow the Holy Spirit would descend on me and I would be brilliant. I wasn't.

You went dashing into the session thinking: "I'll make the call and get it over with." You got the kind of results you deserved.

3. Anxiety

You were nervous, insecure, and uncomfortable. It wasn't an easy visit, and it showed. You had the expression of a person about to undergo root canal surgery.

Chances are almost certain, if you are properly prepared and have practiced, you can overcome your anxiety. There's no reason to be nervous. You know what must be done. You know the drill.

Be at ease. Understand there are those who simply won't be interested in your product no matter how alluring you have made it. That's okay. These folks have a different agenda. It's their loss.

There's nothing you could have done to change their mind. Go on to the next likely buyer.

4. Assuming Too Much

You called on someone you felt knew a good bit more about the product than was actually the case. You jumped to the ask too soon because you assumed too much.

Or you called on someone who had been a good customer for years. You took for granted she'd still be interested in the product.

You felt no need to interpret, to sell the dream, to discuss how important the product is in her life. To ask questions and probe. That's what you thought! You asked for the order too soon. You leaped from step one to step nine. You lose.

5. Failure to Probe

The probable buyer was nodding in approval, smiling, and throwing off all kinds of positive signals during your entire presentation. Even the body language seemed right. You left thinking you had made an invincible case, made the sale.

But you failed to probe for any concerns or determine whether there were lingering questions. You realize that George Bernard Shaw said it all in the title of his wonderful play, *You Never Can Tell*.

You didn't ask the Three Magic Questions. If you don't probe, you haven't even begun to properly prepare to make the ask.

6. Poor Listening

You talked too much, you listened too little. You never found out how the buyer felt about the product because you spent all of your time talking. You failed to "listen the sale."

The more attentive you are in listening to others, the more likely they will listen to you. The more you listen, the more likely they are to embrace your product.

The person asking questions and listening—that's you—is in control of the conversation. Think again of my example of the attorney who examines and probes a witness. The attorney questions, searches, and directs the interrogation and the content of what the judge and jury hear.

The person who listens influences the outcome, not the talker. You are in charge. Listen!

Here's something worth remembering: After 48 hours, a person recollects 37 percent of what you've said. She retains 78 percent of what she's said.

Your job is to ask questions so the answers are actually delivering your sales presentation.

You probe. Let's say, for instance, you're part of the Amway sales force. You are on the team of the world's largest distributor of vitamins, minerals, and nutrients.

You ask: "You seem so interested in these vitamins that provide renewed vitality and health. Tell me, Rebecca, how do you feel about these vitamins and the great results you will have?"

She can't answer a simple *yes* or *no* to this kind of a question. Let her talk. She won't remember what you said. She'll remember the part of your visit when she did the talking. I promise.

7. Too Much on Features and Not Enough on Benefits

You spent your time going over details and speaking about features (this boat is 22 percent more efficient than any other in breaking through the water. Instead, perhaps you should have said something like: "Picture, for a moment, your hands at the wheel of this beauty. The weather is perfect and the boat is cutting through the waves as if . . ."").

You pulled out the fancy brochure and reviewed the specifications of the product. But you failed to notice that the probable buyer's eyes were glazing over.

You spent too much time talking about cost and not enough about the results and outcomes that the buyer could expect from his investment.

The purpose of your presentation isn't to sell a product. It's to help the buyer visualize and enter into his world of the end result.

You didn't take enough time to talk about how the product would enrich his life. There was no magic. You didn't sell the dream. You missed your golden opportunity.

8. Premature Selling

You asked for the order and made a brilliant close. But you didn't take any of the necessary preliminary steps.

You didn't take time to make the product properly irresistible. You didn't probe for concerns or ask enough questions and take time to listen.

You found the likely buyer nodding in agreement and you took that as a sign that you had finished the job. You raced from first to third base, without touching second.

9. Win-Win

It's not an "I win, you lose" game. That's not selling with integrity. In fact, it's selling at its very worst.

It has got to be a win-win proposition. You win because you're meeting your sales objective and there is a commission. That's important, of course, but that's not what drives you.

"You can only be truly accomplished at something you love." You take those words of Maya Angelou to heart. "Don't make money the goal. Pursue something you love doing and do it so well that people can't take their eye off you. The money will come as a result."

You know your product is precisely right for the buyer and will provide great satisfaction. And the buyer wins because the product meets his greatest needs and wishes. There's great joy.

You win. The buyer wins. That's selling with integrity.

10. Didn't Ask

The most heinous sin of all—you didn't ask for the order.

You made a brilliant presentation, you asked all the right questions, you probed. You followed every step. It was a glorious session.

There was one critically important omission. You left before actually asking for the order. You were so pleased with your performance, you forgot the last act.

In my earlier days, I was guilty of this very crime. Actually, in some cases, I was pleased to get out alive without having to make the dreaded ask. I could feel my tongue getting thick, my throat as dry as the Sahara.

If you wait for the perfect time, perfect conditions, the perfect opportunity when everything is just right (and the stars and the moon are in perfect alignment), you'll never ask.

Go ahead. Ask for the order. And take comfort in the fact that it's not the eloquence of your presentation that determines your success or failure. It's the simple act of asking.

One thing is certain—if you don't ask, you won't get the order. It's absolutely amazing what you don't get when you don't ask.

I've composed a little poem to remind you of what happens if you fail to ask for the order.

> A tired and haggard salesman
> Met the Devil at Hell's gate.
> "What have you done," asked Satan,
> "To earn this terrible fate?"
>
> "I don't know," the salesman said,
> "I never shirked a single task.
> I called on every prospect . . . but
> I guess I failed to make the ask."
>
> The Devil showed no mercy,
> With disgust he rang the bell.
> "I condemn you to an eternity," he said,
> "In the fires of deepest hell."

23

Have Only Two Dials on Your Console—Fast and Faster

MAKING THE SALE is often a long process. But most important, you must begin. The only thing guaranteed to stop you from making a sale—is simply not getting started.

I'm reminded that every morning in Africa, a gazelle wakes up. It knows that it must run faster than a lion or it will be killed. Every morning a lion wakes up. It knows it must outrun the slowest gazelle or it will starve to death.

It doesn't matter whether you are a lion or a gazelle—when the sun comes up, you'd better be running.

So you must begin. There are many steps along the way. But in order to make the sale, there are four milestones that play the most significant part. Four steps you must take. I'll give you those in a moment.

It's important you keep the pipeline filled. There can be no let up. You need to have a pool of people you are calling on—new contacts and those you have called on who need following up on.

Let me tell you about Ret Thompson. He sells for Thomas James Custom Clothes. There are 400 regular customers he calls on in his territory in Little Rock, Arkansas.

Just in case you are wondering if the days of house-to-house selling are over—there are more than 500 men and women all over the country just like Ret who represent Thomas James. They call on men and women at their offices and homes to outfit them in custom-made suits, slacks, and shirts.

(In case you're curious if a person can make a good living by making these house calls, just ask Brianne Frey. She sells for Thomas James in New York. In her very first year, she netted $135,419 in commissions.)

Back to Ret. He keeps in contact with his 400 customers on a regular basis. "They never forget who I am. I never let them."

But Ret also cold calls at least one day a week just to keep probable buyers in the pipeline. "It's one of the things I enjoy most. I love telling new people about my wonderful product."

Just like Ret, it's essential you pay special attention to those who have bought your product in the past. You should not spend all of your time chasing new business every day and not taking care of your old friends.

Call your old customers. Find out how satisfied they are. Would they recommend you to friends? Be in regular contact between sales.

And, of course, keep filling the pipeline. Pray for a good harvest, but keep on hoeing.

Here are four steps to help you begin:

1. Make the telephone call to arrange for the visit. (Some of you may have potential customers coming to you. Like in a Wal-Mart, or a shoe store, a Bose outlet, a hardware store—whatever. You won't have to make that difficult call to get the visit.)
2. Meet with the probable buyer face to face to make the presentation. (I've heard it said that the key to a good presentation is to have a brilliant beginning, a dazzling ending—and to keep them as close as possible.)
3. Ask for the order. Keep in mind, if you've done it correctly, you have actually made the sale before you ask for the order.
4. You must get a commitment to something before you leave your meeting—either the sale or a date for another visit.

There may be some intermediate steps along the journey of making the sale—but these four certainly constitute those that stand out and are most important.

Here's what I would like you to do. Assign one point to the first step. You make the telephone call to arrange for the visit.

You receive two points for the second step. You make the call and you get the visit. You make a face-to-face presentation to the probable buyer.

Now, give yourself three points for asking for the order. Whether you make the sale or not, you've taken the essential step. You asked.

And finally, you get four points for the last step. You asked for the order and . . . he said *yes*. You've done it. You made the sale.

Establish a realistic objective, the number of points you feel you can reach. A sober projection. But one that will make you stand on your tiptoes.

If you have a supervisor, the two of you can work on this. It gives you a wonderful way to track your work. Assign yourself the number of points you want to achieve each day, week, and month.

I'll tell you what I did when I first started. I didn't have anything in the pipeline, so I had to start from scratch. I decided I would shoot for 5 points every day, 30 points a week. I was soon meeting and surpassing my objective so I raised my total.

I want you to determine your point objective. If you do this faithfully, you will never run out of buyers, and you will get your work done on a timely basis.

I have found from my personal early experience that the longer you put off making your calls, the more difficult it gets. It's your resolve and determination that assures success.

Accept the challenge and feel the exhilaration. The great dividing line between success and failure can be stated in five words: "I did not get started." It was Clem Stone's favorite admonition to his salespeople: Do it now!

Do it. Just do it. Make your credo TNT—Today Not Tomorrow. It's the start that stops most salespeople.

While you're putting things off, life speeds by. Begin today. There's no perfect time to do something. Do it now. Make the telephone call to arrange for the visit.

I heard an old woodsman from Vermont give this advice about catching a porcupine: "Watch for the slapping tail as you dash in. Grab a large washtub and drop it over him. The washtub will give you something to sit on while you ponder your next move."

The secrets of success do not work unless you do. The successful salesperson is the one who goes ahead and does the thing others never got around to. No statue has ever been erected to the memory of a person who put things off.

So go ahead. TNT! Make your call. Great! You've already earned your first point!

Congratulations, you're a champion. The only things you can be sure of accomplishing are the things you do today. You've made the call. You're on your way to success. You touch the future. You are one of history's handful. You are going to be a supremely successful salesperson.

24

Integrity Isn't Important—It Is Everything

RUDOLF NUREYEV is considered one of the most famous ballet dancers of all time. He is the ultimate *premier danseur*. A friend once said to him, "Rudy—you seem to float in space when you dance. How do you do it?"

"It's easy. All I do is make a flying leap in the air and stay there and never come down."

I am going to give you a formula that's actually easier to implement than the great dancer's leap.

But before I do, I want to discuss with you further the concept of *integrity selling*. I've used the term throughout the book. It's important because credibility is the first law of selling. If you don't believe the messenger, you won't believe the message.

Let me tell you about the derivation of the word, integrity. It comes from the Latin *integritatem*. (This is your Latin lesson for the day.)

Its definition is honesty (as you might expect), trustworthiness, sincerity, and complete openness. That's what I've been advocating throughout these pages.

It means representing your product and company with pride. It means never compromising your ethics. It means the sale must be a win-win. It means you must feel completely fulfilled and rewarded by your profession.

Great salesmanship means you must maintain absolute integrity. That is the beginning and the end of it all.

Know your stuff! Know everything there is to know about your product.

Show uncommon commitment to the buyer. Remember, it's all about them—not you.

Expect positive results. Visualize it. Exhibit your PMA—a positive mental attitude.

Express your passion. Let your buyer know how enthusiastic you are for the product. Let it show.

And now back to how easy it is. The "rights" must all be in place. Here's all it takes.

The Right Person
asks
The Right Probable Buyer
in
The Right Way
at
The Right Time
at
The Right Cost
for
The Right Product
with
The Right Follow-up

See. I told you it would be easy. And, you . . . you are the right person.

Integrity selling says it all. It is where you and the buyer meet at the intersection of a decision, and passion and commitment come alive. You will be a roaring success.

25 | Flimflam Is Out

I'M HAVING COFFEE with Rich DeVos. We're talking about the extraordinary growth of Amway. He tells me that there are 3 million Amway distributors and salespeople all over the world.

Three million! And he says that he has made hundreds of these folks millionaires.

"Tell me," I ask, "how would you sum up your success?"

"It's unbelievably simple," he says. "I tell my salespeople that when they're calling on someone, it's 'the buyer first, *me* second'.

"I'm going to tell you something else. I don't think there are very many who know the story I'm about to tell you.

"When Jay (Jay Van Andel) and I started, we began by buying a sales kit to sell Nutrilite, a food supplement. We knew we wanted to be in business for ourselves and decided that's how we should start.

"Jay sent them a check for 50 dollars to buy the Nutrilite sales kit and some samples. And he had to borrow the money to do that. I didn't even have any money to contribute.

"Well, over the years the business really grew. There was no one else like us. We made a lot of millionaires out of our distributors and salespeople.

"Now here's the part most people don't know.

"Peter Grace came to me one day. He was CEO of the big conglomerate W.R. Grace. It was a powerhouse, one of the largest corporations in the country at that time.

"'We want to buy you,' Grace tells me.

"I tell him we're not for sale.

"'If you don't sell,' he says, 'I'm going to go into the same business and compete against you. And you don't want to go head-to-head with us.'

"I tell him again, we're not for sale. But I tell him I would turn over all of our material and a sample sales kit to him. I'll give him everything he needs to start his new business. I let him know that I think competition is great.

"Well, this giant corporation went into business against us. They used our material and spent a lot of money getting started. But they never really could get it off the ground. After several years of trying and putting a lot of money into it, it collapsed and they closed it down.

"A couple years later, I see Peter Grace in an airport. I say, 'Peter—how's that new program going?' I, of course, know he closed it down.

"He pokes his finger in my chest and says, 'You left out the most important ingredient of all in that material you gave me.'

"'What's that? I ask.

"'Integrity,' he tells me. 'You never told me how important integrity is.'"

Alan Hassenfeld tells me the same thing. "Yesterday, you could get away with flimflam selling. Not today. Today, integrity and ethics count for everything."

If you don't sell with integrity, it is nothing like the real thing. It's a zircon not a diamond.

Doing a thing right and doing the right thing are different. In integrity selling, acquire the habit of both—but cultivate the latter.

Integrity says it all. Aim high. Reach for the stars. You are on your way to being supremely successful.

26 | The Highest of Callings

SELLING WITH INTEGRITY is the highest calling in selling. It is the very foundation in your journey to success.

Integrity selling means there is an equitable transfer of value. You and the buyer both gain in the exchange. Very often the probable buyer will indicate that he or she received a great deal more in purchasing the product than the seller received in making the sale.

Keep in mind that integrity selling isn't something you do to someone. It's something you do for and with someone. Cal Turner tells me that the whole mission in selling throughout his stores is to provide a better life for everyone.

"That's actually in our mission statement," Cal says. "I tell my salespeople—it's not about them, it's about the people who came through our doors. Our job is not to sell them. It's to serve them."

A likely buyer is a real person with concerns, needs, pain, and moments of joy that know no bounds. You are empathetic. You take the necessary time to know your buyer.

It is essential you understand the needs and wants of those you are calling on before you ask them to buy. You develop a trust and a rapport before any asking begins. This could possibly take a number of visits. Don't rush it.

Bonnie McElveen Hunter says you need to be a partner with the buyer. "You've got to connect the needs and desires of your buyer to the product. You are in lock step with the buyer."

You spend enough time with each person and you listen carefully. You know precisely how the negotiations should go and the level of interest on the part of the buyer for your product. You know this by probing and listening. If you can't determine the level of interest in your product, you are not ready to ask for the sale.

Stanley Marcus took me on a tour one day. We left his office for his downtown Dallas store.

When we passed the glove department, we watched a saleswoman discussing various gloves with a customer. We overheard her saying: "I frankly don't think any of these are really right for you. Let me suggest a store that probably has what you have in mind."

Stanley congratulated the saleswoman after the customer left. Congratulated her!

After, Stanley pulled me aside. "We'll have that customer for life. She knows she can trust us. We depend on sales but we would never try to sell something that isn't good for the customer."

Crafty selling techniques give way to buyer-empowering principles. Bonnie McElveen Hunter says she doesn't believe in selling. "You want to set the table so the buyer doesn't have to be sold but is eager to buy."

You develop a high regard for the buyer. There is an unmistakable rapport. Stanley Marcus says that a binding rapport is at the very heart of making a sale. If that type of relationship does not exist—it shows. You can't fake it!

Your high level of integrity contributes more to success in achieving the sale than will bedazzling techniques. You've heard: *close fast, close early, close often*. These are cheap tricks that are an abomination to selling with integrity.

You never exert pressure. If there is any compulsion, and there should be, it is felt by the buyer.

They sense the urgency. They understand how the product will be of immense benefit to them. They anticipate the joy and satisfaction in having the product. It becomes irresistible. The desire builds. The buyer wants or needs the product.

Bonnie McElveen Hunter says: "In the decision to buy, the seller has to make the buyer feel great about the purchase. They need to feel the decision was theirs and that they made a valuable purchase."

The probable buyer may say, "I need to think it over." That may mean she really needs to take time to think it over. You need to probe a bit.

It may mean you haven't answered all their questions. Probe. Go ahead and ask, "Have I answered all your questions and concerns?" Or "Are there still questions you might have?"

What if the buyer says he is not interested? You need to examine what that means. A *no* does not always mean *no*! More often it means: *not just yet*. Ask my Three Magic Questions: Is it the product that's the problem? Is it the cost? Is it the timing?

Hotsy-totsy selling techniques (get them to say yes to a series of questions before you ask for the sale) are superseded by principles and high standards. Relationships build on integrity. This assures successful asking and leaves the buyer with a high level of satisfaction.

You are a salesperson. You are a professional and an ethical motivator.

There are other professions, of course, that provide service and help solve problems. But there is nothing on earth that provides the challenges, personal satisfaction, and the rewards of selling. Yours is the highest of callings.

You are a major piece of the fabric of society. You are persuasive. Poignant. Inspiring.

You move the world forward. You empower others to become happier, more efficient, effective, and successful because of the product you offer and sell. What could be more fulfilling?

I want to grant you the courage to never sell yourself short, grace to risk something bold for something good. And the understanding that the world is too dangerous a place now for anything but truth and integrity.

27 | The Unconquerable Joy of Selling That Ignites a Fire

WHAT YOU ARE about to read next may surprise you.

Felicity and I are having dinner in London not too long ago. We are with the Archbishop of Canterbury. (I apologize for name-dropping, but, well . . . heck!) He heads the worldwide Anglican Communion—including the Episcopal churches in the United States.

We are involved in a major project for the church. The Archbishop is providing his strong leadership to the project. It is a social evening, but it is also to determine the strategy for his proposed program.

"What makes the difference?" I ask. "What makes the difference between a strong, vital parish and one that is faltering and stumbling?"

"That's an easy one," he says. "It's all about leadership.

"If the priest or bishop is strong, the church will flourish. If he or she is weak and languid, the church totters."

"Then tell me, what are the characteristics of a forceful and vital priest?" I'm waiting for a protracted and profound response.

"This is going to surprise you. I've thought about it a lot. What separates the great ones from the insipid and listless priests—are you ready for this—is that the most effective and most highly regarded are having fun in their ministry."

"Having fun? Really?" I would never have guessed this answer.

"Yes, if they're not having fun in their spiritual journey, it shows. The parishioners pick it up right away. The priest may be lyrical in providing the liturgy and give a thundering sermon. That won't count. There's got to be great joy in his life. You can't bluff joy."

You may well wonder how applicable a church analogy is to selling. Let me explain.

If you think for a moment that being a priest, minister, or rabbi doesn't involve the ability to motivate, empathize, inspire, relate effectively to people, and at some point ask for the order—then you, my friend, don't understand or know the church!

Let me tell you about a characteristic I find in all of the great salespeople I know and have coached. They love their work. No matter how irksome and oppressive the day, they still have fun along the way. They have more fun than a van full of clowns and jugglers.

"If it's not fun, it's not worth all the effort." That's what Bonnie McElveen Hunter tells me.

"When we have a customer coming to our office, we pull out all the stops. It's like we're putting on a party for them. The whole staff is having fun and the customer knows it." Bonnie would probably bring out the marching band if that would help.

The supremely successful salesperson is willing to pay the price—whatever the cost. Their work becomes something of an obsession. It burns like fire in their bones. This could be onerous if it wasn't also fun.

You need to feel like the marvelously talented tennis player, Venus Williams. She was asked why she keeps on playing competitive tennis. "It's what I love to do. It has given me a wonderful and special life. And it's just plain fun."

You've heard the dictum: No pain, no gain. Success is a moving target. Often, a salesperson can feel a bit like Odysseus, the hero of Homer's *Odyssey*; "My life is endless trouble and chaos."

There are the long hours, long days, some of which seem never to end. But still there is joy and exhilaration, fulfillment, and an inner glow. It's just plain fun.

You know the feeling. You made the sale. You are floating in space. You are completing a sequence of *fouettés*, ending with a triple *pirouette*.

Even if you don't make the sale, there's a whole world of people out there waiting for you to call on them. You follow Frank Sinatra's refrain: "You pick yourself up and get back in the race."

When you think about it, the reason is obvious. Selling has the power to dramatically impact society in a way no other profession can. It makes the world go around. And you're an integral part of that noble pursuit.

Northwestern Life Insurance is one of the largest underwriters in the nation. The Nashville regional office led the country for years in sales. William Cochran headed the office and was consistently one of the company's leading salesmen.

I ask Bill one day if there is one thing he could think of that is a common thread woven through all of his outstanding insurance salespeople. Is it persistence? I ask. A great communicator? Hard worker? A good listener? What is it?, I ask.

"All of those are essential, and there are other qualities, also. But that's not it," Bill tells me. "I notice that among the very most productive, they're having fun.

"I can tell fairly soon if one of my people is not going to make it. I don't even have to look at their sales records. It's obvious they're not having fun. I sit down with them and tell them they ought to be doing something else, something they would enjoy."

Happiness and having fun in your work are the unsurpassed of all riches. And best of all, they're not taxed. Selling isn't really work unless you would rather be doing something else.

"Try a thing four times." That's the advice Stanley Marcus gave me.

"Once to get over the fear of doing it. The second time to learn how to do it. Successfully. The third time to figure out whether you like it or not. And finally, have fun doing it."

Psst. Here's the lesson. Along the way, have fun. It is the music of the soul. It shows and it's contagious. Selling should be a vast and indolent fecundity. A perpetual samba!

28 | You Don't Have to Be Great to Start, But You Have to Start to Be Great

HERE ARE MY GOLDEN RULES of selling with integrity. These are the principles we've covered in the book. This is the catechism of successful selling according to Panas.

"Begin at the beginning," said the king bravely in *Alice in Wonderland*, "and go on until you come to the end. Then stop."

1. Begin by knowing everything possible about your product, its many uses, the features that are unique to it—its extraordinary benefits, everything.
2. Make certain, in your heart-of-hearts, you're completely committed to the worthiness and advantage of the product. If you're not passionate about what you're offering, it will show.

   Worse than that, if you aren't intensely certain of its value, it's a scam. And that's not integrity selling.

   It must be far more than an intellectual conviction. It must be deeply felt in your heart-of-hearts—and even a presence in your dreams.
3. You need to get going. You must begin.

   There are two ways to get to the top of an oak tree. One way is to sit on an acorn and wait. The other is to climb the tree.
4. Work hard. Keep at it. Never let up.

   Yes, I know. I've heard it, also. You must work smarter, not harder. I suggest you do both.

   I suggest you only work half a day. It makes no difference which half. It can either be the first 12 hours on the last 12 hours.
5. Learn everything you can about the likely buyer you'll be calling on and his buying history.
6. After careful assessment, determine the specific product you will be presenting. That takes probing and asking questions.
7. Give some thought as to how you'll express the cost of the product. Say it out loud several times before your visit.

8. If your selling entails contacting and calling on people, keep in mind that 85 percent of making the sale is setting the visit. When you call for the visit, don't get cornered into trying to make the case or attempt to make the sale on the telephone. Make it brief and set the schedule for the visit.

9. Practice, practice, practice. Write out what you're going to say when you call for the visit.

10. Write out in advance all of the reasons your probable buyer may try to put you off. Practice how to respond.

11. Call first on those most likely to buy.

12. Keep in mind what's most important to the buyers you call on: *empathy, energy, enthusiasm*, and *ethics*. Remember, Mary Kay tells us that what your probable buyer wants is key: "Make me feel important."

13. It's important, in the first few minutes, to gain their interest and attention. You have them in your embrace. Getting their attention is essential.

    A man saw another man beating a donkey. He approached him and asked why he was beating the animal. "I want him to move, but he won't," said the donkey's owner.

    "You just have to reason with him," said the other. "May I try?"

    "Sure," the donkey's owner said. So the man picked up a brick and hit the donkey on the head with it.

    "I thought you were going to reason with him," the owner said.

    "I am, but first I have to get his attention."

14. During the visit, use your early moments to establish rapport and common ground. Take as much time as necessary. But remember, your objective is to talk about the product and make the sale.

15. In your discussion, be completely honest about the product. This means putting every word on trial for its life. That's selling with integrity.

16. It is essential that you probe for concerns—anything that might delay or derail the sale.

17. Ask open-ended questions.

18. Listen. Malin Burnham says he's reminded that he read somewhere that it's better to keep one's mouth shut most of the time and be thought a fool than to open it and resolve all doubt.

19. Take no more than seven minutes to present the product and its irrefutable value. Use less time if possible. The buyer wants to know the answers to these questions: (a) Why should I buy this product? (b) What's in it for me— how do I benefit? (c) Why should I buy it now? (d) Why should I buy from you?

20. Convey the great benefit to the buyer. It has to be a win-win for both you and the buyer. If it's not a win for the buyer, it's not integrity selling. Honesty and integrity aren't the most important elements that count in making a sale—they're the only thing that counts.

21. Don't sell features. Talk about outcomes and results.

22. Give testimony to your own use of the product and talk about others who have used the product.

23. When finally asking for the order, use words such as: "I would like you to consider purchasing . . ."

24. Wait for a response. Don't fill in the silence—no matter how long it seems to take. It's what John Updike once called: "A painful, agonizing silence."

25. Don't let objections rattle you. They are your best friends. Probe for concerns. If you don't, you will not know how the probable buyer really feels about the product.

Some people are always grumbling because roses have thorns. Instead they should be thankful those thorns have roses. Objections are not the thorns. They are the roses.

If there is an objection, I like to ask in an easy and nonthreatening way: "I believe I understand your concern. And we'll get back to that. But I'm just curious—is there any other reason that might prevent you from taking advantage of my offer today?" This is an excellent way to draw out any other objections, if there are any.

26. Use the Three Magic Questions. Is it the product? Is it the cost? Is it the timing?

27. Get a commitment to something before leaving, either the sale or the date for another visit.

28. Don't let the cost dominate the discussion—even though that may be a major stumbling block. Remember, most sales will not be lost because of cost. The product must have intrinsic value to the buyer and serve her needs and fulfill her dream.

29. From the very beginning, be positive. Think success. If you can conceive it, you can achieve it—remember that in all you do.

And there you have it. My 29 principles. They are the grammar of supremely successful selling. There are not 28 and there aren't 30. But follow these 29 rules and it will forever affect the way you do your selling.

I can perhaps be challenged on some of these items. But I do feel a bit like Alfred Austin, poet laureate at the turn of the last century. He referred to his divine inspiration. "I dare not offer these things as being my own. They come to me from above."

You will be vastly successful—beyond your wildest dreams. That's a promise. You're going to be great.

29 | Here's the Magic

"WHERE AM I?"

"In the hall."

"Where do I want to be?"

"In that man's office."

"What will happen if I go inside?"

"The worst is I'd be thrown back out in the hall."

"Well, that's where I am now, so what have I got to lose?"

Have you ever had that conversation with yourself? I have. I know what it's like to have the dreaded disease—*doorknob phobia*.

The first few calls I made were horrifying. It was like opening a vein. That's because I had no idea what to do. I strutted through the first part of the presentation and staggered through the last.

I made plenty of mistakes. I could identify with A. A. Milne's Winnie the Pooh. He wrote: "Here is Edward Bear, coming downstairs now, bump, bump, bump, on the back of his head. It is as far as he knows, the only way of coming downstairs, but sometimes he feels there really is another way, if he could stop bumping for a moment and think of it."

You will likely make some mistakes, also. Just like Edward Bear, look for another way.

You may try and fail, but don't fail to try. If you conquer doubt and fear, you conquer failure.

As Sir Edmund Hillary said, when he conquered Mount Everest, "You never conquer the mountain. You only conquer yourself."

I've learned that it's more an art than a science, but a glorious combination of both. There are different ways to make the sale.

Let me tell you about a newly hired traveling salesman. He wrote his first sales report to the home office. It was shocking.

It was obvious that the new salesperson was ignorant. Here's what he wrote:

"I seen this outfit which they ain't never bought a dime's worth of nothing from us and I sole them som goods. I'm now goin' to Chicawgo."

His supervisor was ready to fire the new salesman. Then came his letter from Chicago:

"I caym hear and sole them haff a million."

What to do? The sales manager was afraid of firing the ignorant salesman, but wasn't sure. He gave the problem to the president to solve.

The following morning, members of the sales department were amazed to see a memo from the president. It was posted on the bulletin board above the two letters written by the ignorant salesman. The president wrote:

"We ben spending two much time trying to spel instead of tryin' to sel. Let's watch those sails. I want everybody should read these letters from Homer Gooch who is on the rod doin' a grate job for us and you should go out and do like he done."

I can still remember the first sale I ever made. I felt I was getting close. It had gone wonderfully well, everything according to the script. I was at that moment in the discussion when it was time to ask for the order.

I wanted to say: Here's the contract and once it's committed, signed, notarized, and entered at the County Courthouse, I'll give you back the keys to your car!

But I didn't. I asked properly and made the sale. And to my delight, the buyer was as pleased as I was.

Here's what I learned. I thought about Dumbo. He thought he got airborne with the help of a magic feather. But just remember. Dumbo didn't need the feather. The magic was in him.

I realized . . . I realized, the magic is in me.

I learned what glorious fun and how important this could be, this mission of selling. I loved it. I realized that through my efforts, I was actually helping to touch lives in a very special way.

Everyone sells, whether they know it or not. The minister, the doctor, the receptionist, the attorney, the classroom teacher. Some are more successful at it than others. But in their own way, they are all selling.

In selling a product you make the world go around. If it weren't for the salespeople, all commerce would come to a standstill. We are the engine that powers the train.

When I'm selling, I am making it happen, I'm soaring. What's that old refrain: "I'm flying higher than a kite and my feet don't touch the ground. And I'm loving the state I'm in." You're going to feel this way, too.

Me, I have a fantasy. I'm at those beautiful pearly gates. St. Peter is looking down at me. There's a long questionnaire in his hands. "And what did you do that we should let you in?" he asks in a deep baritone.

I tell St. Peter I've been helping a lot of people—I'm a salesman. I'm a crusader for important products.

A smile crosses his face. "Come in," he says, "we've been expecting you."

Lucky you. You are a salesperson. Some shy away. Some are afraid. Some say they don't like it. You know better. You are, in your own special way, helping change a corner of the world.

You are what F. Scott Fitzgerald meant when he wrote, "We couldn't do without you. You are the greatest of them all."

Appendix

The Dozen Objections to Getting the Visit

These are the type of objections you are most likely to get when you call for your visit. You may have one or two to add—but I doubt it!

I've included just about everything I can think of. And I've encountered just about all of them.

Here's what I want you to do. Study these objections. Have a response in mind for each one. You will most likely hear one of them.

Remember: Your job is to secure the visit. If you get to see your customer, you're 85 percent on your way to getting the order. I guarantee it.

Have these objections by the phone—with your responses. Go ahead. Make the call. You're on your way.

1. Now is not a good time for me. I'm terribly busy.
2. I can give you 10 minutes, maybe15. No more than that.
3. I don't think I'm really interested in your product.
4. Why don't you tell me on the phone what you're selling? That would save us both a lot of time instead of having a visit.
5. Why don't you send me some material? I'll look it over and if I'm interested, I'll send you an order.
6. I'm pretty much committed to another product much like yours.
7. I used your product once and didn't have a very good experience. I don't think I'd be interested in a visit.
8. I do most of my buying through Amazon and the Internet.
9. My spouse makes these decisions in our family. I'm probably not the right person to talk with.
10. I don't have any money left. I'm not certain a visit would be very helpful for either of us.
11. I'm simply not interested in your product. I think a visit would be a waste of your time.
12. What is this going to cost me? I need to know before I arrange to see you.

Overcoming the Dozen Challenges to Getting the Order

You have asked for the order. You are quite likely to get some objections. You can count on it.

There may be more objections, but these dozen challenges are pretty much what you're going to hear. Be prepared.

There's a perfect answer. Work on it. Do this before the visit when you ask for the order.

Keep in mind, if you get the visit, you are 85 percent on your way to making the sale. Remember the Three Magic Questions—is it the product, the amount, or the timing? When you find that out, you're on your way.

One thing more. Your objective is not to knock down the objection. You respond in a thoughtful, compelling way: "I understand how you feel . . ."

1. I'm not certain I can answer right now. I'll need to think it over.
2. That's a lot of money you're talking about.
3. It's a great product, but your timing is lousy. This hasn't been a good year for me.
4. I'll need time to think this over. Give me some time to think about it and I'll get back to you.
5. It's way more than I would consider paying.
6. What kind of assurance do I have that your product will do everything you claim?
7. I believe in what you're selling. I just wish you had come sooner. I've just made a significant purchase.
8. This is the kind of thing I need to talk over with my spouse.
9. You make a good case. Your presentation was interesting. I like your product. But I have a number of salespeople who call on me. There's only so much I can do and I'm already pretty much committed.
10. I've been pretty satisfied with what I've been using.
11. I don't see how your product is going to make a difference for me.
12. The truth is, I still have a lot of questions about the product.

Sample Letter Using a Reference

Ken B. Smart
199 Maple Court
Stanford, Connecticut 04013

Dear Mr. Sample:

You are a good friend and colleague of Bob Sample. He suggested I call you.

Bob has been using our product for some time. We just came out with a new version—and he is particularly pleased with it. "The best I've ever had," he told me.

He thought you would be as excited and enthusiastic about our new version as he is. I'm pretty certain you will be.

I'll be calling you in the next few days to arrange a time for a visit. Bob has told me so much about you. I do look forward to greeting you in person.

Sincerely,
Ken B. Smart

Sample Letter Requesting a Visit

Bobbi Selz
347 Marchand Street
Kokomo, Indiana 46901

Dear Sarah and Sam:

I'll be calling in the next few days to set a time when we might visit. I want to tell you about a very exciting product that will make a significant difference in your home and in your life.

I believe you are going to find this as exciting as many of your neighbors have. I'll share some names of some happy customers when I see you.

On this visit, I'm not going to be asking you to buy the product. That's a promise. If the two of you decide to do something later on, that will be entirely up to you.

I do look forward to the visit. I'll be calling in the next few days.

Sincerely,
Bobbi Selz

Sample Letter Confirming a Visit

Bobbi Selz
347 Marchand Street
Kokomo, Indiana 46901

Dear Peter:

Thanks so much for arranging for our visit.

I'll be at your home next Wednesday evening at 7 P.M. Let's plan on no more than an hour together.

I'm really looking forward to being with you and Mary.

Sincerely,
Bobbi Selz

About the Author

In one of his books, the author wrote:

"Someone once told me that my career would have five stages:

1. Who is Jerry Panas?
2. Get me Jerry Panas,
3. We need someone like Jerry Panas,
4. What we need is a young Jerry Panas, and,
5. Who is Jerry Panas?"

Jerry believes he's somewhere between stages two and three. "But," he says, "my friends indicate I'm somewhere in Stage Four, quickly approaching Stage Five!"

He is considered the high-priest of personal motivation and one of the nation's most formidable platform presenters on success and winning. His seminars pack the house.

Jerry is the author of thirteen books, many of them classics in the field. He's also a feature columnist, a popular sales coach, and one of the nation's foremost exporters of enthusiasm and positive mental attitude.

He is the senior officer of one of America's premier firms that empowers men and women to more fully utilize their innate talents and hone their skills and techniques.

Jerry says that selling is part science and part art. He combines the two in a wonderful mixture that ensures success.

For information about speaking engagements, e-mail: ideas@jeroldpanas.com.

Index

211